THE END OF EDEN

THE END OF EDEN

Writings of an Environmental Activist

by Thomas Rain Crowe

with illustrations by Robert Johnson

WIND PUBLICATIONS
2008

International Standard Book Number 978-1-893239-80-7
Library of Congress Control Number 2008929154

First edition

Illustrations and cover art by Robert Johnson.

The author thanks the editors of the following publications in which
some of the articles and essays in this collection have previously appeared: *Smoky Mountain News, Wild Mountain Times, Katuah Journal,
Eco-logic, The Sylva Herald, Heartstone, Asheville Citizen-Times,
Cashiers Chronicle, Salamander, Mountain Xpress, Black Mountain
Review, Nantahala Review,* Elemental South (UGA Press), *New Southerner.*

"The Idiot's Wind" was written and first performed by the author for
the *Air Aid* concert in Asheville, NC in August of 2005. It first appeared in print as a broadside published by New Native Press.

"May It Continue" originally appeared in *Zoro's Field: My Life in the
Appalachian Woods*, University of Georgia Press, in 2005.

"Planting Corn" was first published in a collection of poems titled *New
Native* by New Native Press in 1993.

for Robert Zahner, woodsman (1923–2007)

and the residents of Jackson County, N.C.

List of Illustrations

Contents

III. TALES FROM THE TAILGATE MARKET
(Columns)

"The gradual conquest of Europe by the Judeo-Christian worldview changed [the landscape]. The sacred places were broken up, plowed under, cut down. Christian preachers carrying the messages of Paul, Jerome, and Augustine went through the countryside of the Old World, exorcising it, desacralizing it, taming it. In their wake the only officially recognized sacred places were churches, cathedrals, and Christian shrines."

— Frederick Turner
Spirit of Place: The Making of an American Landscape

Preface

"I am the depository of song. I am the reader.
I love the sprigs and the compact wattling."
— Taliesin

For the last few years since the publication of my nature memoir *Zoro's Field: My Life in the Appalachian Woods*, people have been asking me "What are you writing now? When's your next book coming out?" For the longest time, I didn't have a response to their questions. Now, with *The End of Eden*, I can finally say that there is something tangible I can offer those who have inquired about the "sequel" to *Zoro's Field* as well as to the nature of my life following my years in the woods.

I can remember reading Thoreau's *Walden* for the first time and wondering afterwards what Thoreau had done AFTER he came out of the woods. How did he spend the rest of his life? And what was the impact of the Walden Pond experience on the years that followed? In Thoreau's case, we have lots of sources to draw from in answering these questions. In my case, after leaving Zoro's field and the woods of the Green River watershed, my personal history is, for the most part, documented in my writing. In essays, articles, editorials and columns that I have written for local and regional publications and papers here in western North Carolina.

Between the covers of this book, then, lies the evidence of my literary and journalistic efforts over the period of the past twenty years or so—since I left my "bee loud glade" in the woods next to Zoro's field. In this sense, my life and my writing follow the narrative path of an environmental activist working in the guise of a news reporter and free-lance writer who attempts to uplift and enlighten the general public about the issues of preservation of natural resources, regional cultural history and bioregional ethics. For many years, this meant being the proverbial "voice in the wilderness" with little or no attention being paid to my editorials and little action being taken on the ground. More recently, that scenario has changed.

These, then, are essays, articles and editorials focusing on place, and specifically the Smoky Mountain region of western North Carolina. Keying in on its environmental trials and tribulations, this book deals with various bioregional ideas, themes and issues which are appropriately akin to this place, but which can also serve as a microcosm for many of the rural areas of this country that, like these mountains, are experiencing devastating consequences of overpopulation and disfiguring development. I would like to think I have written a kind of handbook for those who might see themselves as wanting to write about the environment to make a difference in the locale in which they live. A handbook, as well, for those who wish to find inspiration for taking on the powers that be where they live and doing "the real work," as Gary Snyder would call it, of grassroots organizing and "rallying the troops." While this is only the model of one man's attempts at saving his homeland from mindless hedonism, outside invasion, and outright denial, I am hoping that there might be enough "universal truth" in what I write to be of some use to others experiencing similar incursions in their own locales.

One of my teachers and mentors (and a name you will see referenced often in the writing in this book) is a man named Thomas Berry. Thomas's work on global sustainability and environmental preservation is, in my mind, unparalleled in the contemporary canon of eco-writing and thought. In his work, he writes about the importance of writing and writers to the Environmental Movement. "Literature must always be one of the main sources of guidance as well as a main source of psychic energy for the task of renewal. Now, in the face of global devastation, it is important that we have a literature that is more intimate and responsive to the natural world. One that gives us images of co-existence and nurturing. And the poets first of all can help provide us with this sort of mystical imperative or directive." These words have, over the years, given me a kind of poetic license to go forward with the work of literary activism and environmental protection. In a world where globalization has usurped notions of local and regional autonomy and stewardship, Berry's use of the words "nurturing" and "intimate" stand out strongly in this statement and in his work in general. I have taken these terms to heart and in my own writing I have tried to be intimate and responsive toward my subject matter and to the people to whom I write. In the end, I would like to think that somewhere my writing and my work on behalf of The Environment has found a place. Its place. I know (from what I have been told) that some of what I have had to say over the years and on specific issues has made more than a small difference to the people and the place in which I live. Beyond this, I can only hope that I may have made some small contribution to the eco-writers' tradition and to the future of the planet and humankind.

To end, let me just say a few brief words about some of my influences for writing this book, as well as make a short speech on the subject of *diversity*. I was lucky enough to have been involved in the foundational days of the Bioregional Movement on the west coast of California during the 1970s, working with and around people like Peter Berg of *Planet Drum*, Lee Swenson of *Simple Living*, poet Gary Snyder, and others. What I learned from that time and those people was that diversity is the sustaining concept throughout all of nature, and, in fact, the universe. It is, in the end, diversity which sustains the quality of life for all living things, allowing everything to survive and to evolve, to continue. It was impressed upon me in those youthful days that once the idea or, worse, the reality of a monogenic mentality or monoculture takes root, everything starts to look like everything else around it—the gene pool is weakened, and the quality of life is compromised. Diversity, for me, is essential in both a philosophical and a practical way. It is essential to the natural world—meaning it is also essential to the human world. I think it's a wonderful thing that we have different cultures and different peoples, different races, different languages and belief systems. If this kind of diversity didn't exist, life as we know it wouldn't exist. And, maybe, neither would we.

3

Life would be fairly dull, don't you think, if we were all the same color, and there was only one variety of tree, one kind of snake or salamander, and one way to think of or worship God? In this kind of mono-world, our imaginations (which are essentially fueled by the natural world and the diversity and mystery of the Universe) would go flat, dry. Entropy would set in. We would cease to be the creatures we are. Having had my eyes opened to this kind paradigm of diversity, and at the same time being witness to the pandemic of globalization and mono-cultural thinking, it is easy for me to say, now, and with conviction, that I am not willing to live in a world absent of elephants and whales. Let me say it again: I am not willing to live in a world absent of elephants and whales!

I

YOU MUST GO HOME AGAIN

Essays

Trrchaptum biforme?
Tough
flesh

Dutchmans Pipe

vine

Frazier
magnolia
bud

Striped
maple
bud

Black
birch
Fruiting
catkin

From old
squaws
root or
bear corn
growing
in
clumps

old
Tree
snail
shell

40'-50'
Chineese
chestnuts
around the
cabin

Black Mountains
in back

Blue Ridge Pkwy.
Old Ballew Cabin

1/8/07

Robert Johnson

Triple Negatives
Losing a Language

The speech of the Southern Mountaineers bristles with strong language, pungent metaphors, vivid similes, and vigorous per-sonifications—"beastifications"—that are tricks of language that have in many instances served the highlander and his an-cestors since before Chaucer.
    — Cratis Williams, *Mountain Life & Work*, 1962

Love of place and love of language go hand in hand. Or, as my old friend Zoro once said, "Who you are is all about where you are from." As a boy growing up over in Graham County, my first language was what has been called "Southern Mountain Speech"—a rich blend of Scots, Chaucerian English, and a witty Irish lyrical structure when spoken coming from Scotland and Ireland. This Appalachian dialect was inherently rich with poetic idioms and colloquialisms, lyrical inflections and natural rhythms, making it unique as well as almost incomprehensible to any outsider. I can still remember a rainy Saturday in the Snowbird Supply General Store in Robbinsville and an old fella talking about the same summer thunder storm that had me and my buddies holed up inside drinking RC Colas and eating Moon Pies, and him calling the storm a "sizzly sod-soaker." And later during those years hearing references to such "thundery weather" as "a Devil's footwasher" and a "nubbin' stretcher." There was no lack of colorful speech. Surrounded by such language, it's no wonder that as early as the third grade I had already become interested in poetry, and by the fourth grade was writing my own.

But during the summer of 1962, my parents moved our family out of Milltown in Robbinsville to the northern end of the Blue Ridge

Parkway just west of Charlottesville, Virginia—thus segregating me from the culture and the language I had grown up with.

Moving away from the place where I had consciously begun to identify and know myself was nothing less than a kind of "removal." A forced march. My own "trail of tears."

As I said my goodbyes to my Cherokee and Scots-Irish friends and my life in the Mountain South along Snowbird Creek in Graham County and the particular, if not peculiar, culture there, little did I know that I was also saying goodbye to a tradition and the way I linguistically viewed the world.

As my father uprooted our family, time and time again in a march of migration further and further north, with each move I lost more and more of my contact and association with my cultural roots. By the time I had finished high school in the steel town of Bethlehem, Pennsylvania, I had become little more than a rolling stone—one that had not had time enough in any one place to gather moss. And as years went by, and as I moved myself farther and farther west on my own, I effectively learned to distance myself from any semblance of a southern accent—so strong were the prejudices I encountered from people from other parts of the country against "southern speech." Tired of being castigated and denigrated, I taught myself a generic American speech that was dialect-free and therefore without character—a final act of acculturation.

Even though I continued to write poetry, it had become a poetry unaffected by place as far as language was concerned. Instead of the organic lyrical and idiomatic poetry that might have come easily had I remained in Graham County, I was, by the time I was twenty-five, writing in rhetorical rhythms a kind of message-based poetry more influenced by Russia and France than by the Mountain South. People who met me were always astonished that I had come from "the South," so well had I hidden my past in my newly-formed language and speech. Only once can I recall slipping and falling back into grace—during the time when I was living an apprentice's life in San Francisco surrounded by many of my Beat generation idols—on the occasion of meeting a young musician from Berea, Kentucky named Wayde Blair in a North

Beach cafe. Because of his strong southern drawl, I reverted back to old speech patterns which had become buried in my subconscious, but which had broken ground almost instantly upon hearing his voice and the familiar language. I would, I was told (for I was totally unaware of the shift in my speech at the time), lapse into dialect and even old Appalachian metaphoric idioms when I would run into Wayde and we began talking casually about "home" and "the past." Aside from these few San Francisco slips, I was and remained dialect free.

To make a long story short, I am back here in western North Carolina again, many years after leaving the region as a young teenager. Now, the cultural life, as well as the language, is dying out, as more and more of my generation have moved to larger towns in the region or further to the north, south or west to search for greater prosperity. One can only hear good old Southern Mountain Speech from the elderly, who have decreased in number as each year has passed. This being the case, upon returning to the western North Carolina mountains, I found myself gravitating towards and spending time with the old folks like Zoro and Bessie Guice, Mose Bradley and Gelolo McHugh over in Polk County, and more recently, Claude and Mary Jane Queen, here in Jackson County. But now, in my late fifties, my recall of my native tongue is faulty, if not almost non-existent, as I taught myself too well, over the years while I was gone, how to speak *sans* dialect. And no matter how hard I try to converse on an equal basis with my sept- and octogenarian friends, I am only able to give lip service to my former language.

Here in the mountain farming community of Tuckasegee,[1] where I now live, I have been moved to try to return to my cultural and linguistic roots and to incorporate these back into my daily speech as well as into my writing. Since moving to Jackson County, I have continued my habit of spending time with members of the elder generation as well as the remaining few of my own age who have held tight to traditions, culture and speech harkening back to the past. In addition to those

---

[1] The community is spelled Tuckasegee, the river is Tuckaseigee, other spellings include Tuckaseegee, from the Cherokee "daksi-yi" (pronounced "dahkshi-yi") which means Turtle Place.

between my Little Canada neighbors and myself over the years, there have, also, been many memorable conversations with characters such as now-deceased Cherokee medicine-man Amoneeta Sequoyah and historian/arts dealer Tom Underwood over on the Qualla Boundary.

There have been many such colorful conversations as this over the years with younger generation story-tellers ("yarn-spinners") such as Paul Rhodes of the Saluda/Fork Creek Rhodes, and Keith Monteith—of the Fontana/Cullowhee Monteiths—whose "lickety cut" mind and quick wit, when coupled with their mountain drawl, has caused me to "rar" back in my boots with laughter, or a broad smile.

Since returning to the mountains of my boyhood, I've attempted to re-establish my identity, my sense of belonging to a particular place and culture, by utilizing Southern Mountain Speech in innovative and creative ways, mainly through my writing. While it may be true, meta-phorically and metaphysically, that *you can't go home again*, the fact is that I HAVE come home again and am finding that I can call up the past in bits and pieces and bring it into the present-day voice in which I write. Can pull up, like from a Chaucerian computer, the triple nega-tives, the "don't make no neverminds" and the "not nary a any's" to lyrically grace the images that my poems and my fictions address.

During the winter months, when I have concentrated time and en-ergy to read and write at length, in poems with titles such as "A Beatnik Wanders Into Appalachia and Learns the Language of Earth and Sky," "Crack-Light," and "Who-Shot-John," I've been able to re-live the past as well as to bring it to light (life) and into the present for myself. When I write "Dig the Big-Eyed Bird in swag or hollow/of locust and locked wood," I am back in Graham County on the mountain behind my family's little house in the Milltown community along Snowbird Creek, and, at the same time, I am here along the Tuckaseigee River experiencing a kind of time-travel generated by language—a leap of almost fifty years. When I write "I make a match to this wick of words" and I can feel strength and satisfaction coming from the heart. In these moments it seems as if I've got the best of both worlds: past and pres-ent.

As a gardener of both legumes and language, I know that a time will come when I'll have to lay down my hoe, and my pen, forever. But until that day comes, I aim to keep on diggin'. Harvesting the bounty afforded me by good organic food and this beautiful Southern mountain speech.

Here With Who-Shot-John *

for Jim Wayne Miller and Jonathan Williams

Come here where the nary and neverminds
don't give a shuck or a jive
'bout the bees in the branch or
the billies in the blind that
come clear, come hell or high water
and dabble down at the spring house
where the ducks lay their eggs
and I write.

Here where the burnt-out dog lies
on the porch bull-raggin the bugs
til he is bit and bawls like a lunk-head
and lopes down the yard and
through the garden greens and taters
til he is out of sight.

Here where the beauty of the hills
holds sway over my pricey thoughts and
my puny pen makin' its way across paper
like it was a goat in the grass
goin' nigh into the newground that
we cleared this week for more corn.

Here where this night in my noggin
names notions that no furriner ever knew
and no gabby gal ever let slip from
her sweet tongue that wouldn't melt butter
or swaller no shine.

Here in this creekbed of moonlight whar
a wetrock won't even sharpen my words,
woozy and wrangled from Who-shot-John
and I wrastle with the devil in the winder
like an old windbag
who is pert-nigh petered out
and wild outen his eyes.

* *colloquialism of Southern Mountain speech for "moonshine"*

You Must Go Home Again

...and he remembered how these sounds, coming to him from the river's edge in the little town of his boyhood, had always evoked for him their tongueless prophecy of wild and secret joy, their glorious promises of new lands, morning, and a shining city. But now the lonely cry of the great train was speaking to him with an equal strangeness of return. For he was going home again.

— Thomas Wolfe, *You Can't Go Home Again*

After I left western North Carolina and then the Blue Ridge mountains in the summer of 1968, I spent many years traveling and living north and westward across the U.S. and abroad, moving away from my past and certain limitations I had been led to believe were inherent in my Smoky Mountain Appalachian upbringing, looking always for "greener pastures," brighter sunsets, and a 1960s-tinted utopia. As it turned out, the grass was greener, here, all along. But it took many years and many miles for me to see western North Carolina for what it was: the place I was looking for, and home.

Now, with the beginning breaths of the new millennium already under our belts, and in response to Thomas Wolfe's anguished cry of "you can't go home again" canonized during the first half of this century, I would like now to say "you Must go home again!" By "home" I mean the idea of an awareness and inner, soulful loyalty to sense of place, and more literally to a particular place—a place in Nature—a point of geography where one resides with reverence and respect, where one's heart and brain are filled, Zen-like, with the silences as well as the sounds of life, in the rural woodlands and in the urban streets, and is at peace. I am speaking, here, about that place where one gathers into his or her body the conscious and unconscious knowledge of the ancient history of that place. The religious and cultural background of what has, in fact, gone on there before him or her. A place where that more ancient history becomes a part of them and with that as a solid foundation they can grow in that place, like any tree... Usually, these kinds of places, for most of us, are places where we spent time as children. These seem to be the places we know best. Instinctively. Intuitively. In this sense, perhaps *home* is who we are. Where we are really from. Deep inside.

On the other hand, we are a mobile, migratory people. And in that sense, *home* is a relative term used, often, to describe migration routes along which we have spent little time in any one place. With regard to this scenario, how, then, do we identify place in terms other than those given to us by the few who have remained in one place over the course of a lifetime?

During my years on the road, I had the opportunity to visit and live in places that were self-identified as "new communities." These were, for the most part, communities of people who had moved back to the land, coming from the larger urban centers on both coasts. But even here, in these small pockets of "higher consciousness" and intellectual and artistic example, where trends, ideas, and alternative patterns of lifestyle were being set for the whole country, there was yet something missing. Even though an understanding had been reached on intellectual levels, and year by year these communities were learning to cope with the environment more and more efficiently, there still was a feeling of displacement—a sort of frantic rush to understand rather than a strong and yet serene sense of surrender.

Perhaps it is possible for some to adopt a home along the migration route of their lives, and for some who come from impossible urban environments or ultra-rural regions short on employment, even a necessity. But if that home is more an idea, a social philosophy, a religion, rather than a geographical area which lingers close to one's heart and which inspires his or her passions and imagination, gives wind to his or her wings, and puts water on his or her tongue, then it is not truly one's home.

In my mind, that sense of surrender, of giving in or over to, is the difference between a true sense of place and a posture of pretending that incorporates only the idea of *sense of place* into one's life. The idea, finally, must come down and rest, at peace, in the body—come to rest in the feet as they stand, firmly, on solid ground. And only the place, the right place, itself, can give us this feeling, this sense of being "at home," where silence is not a threat and noise not an irritation or a plague.

As I see it, and after all the years I spent on the road, we must go home again, take the knowledge, the experience and the strength gained from all the years of wandering, searching, working, and plant this in the soil of our adopted or original homes wherever they may be. We must take our ideas, our dreams, our children, back to where we are really from.

For some of us (as it was in my case) our hometowns, our home-lands, need to be saved from unchecked and rampant development (condominiums, gated communities, second homes, fast food estab-lishments, corporate merchandising warehouses) which has insinuated itself on our region during our absence. This is work to be done. For some of us, we have returned to find that the educational institutions and systems have lain fallow and need to be updated and improved. This is new work that needs be done. For others of us the ecological balance of our public parks (old growth forests, national wilderness areas) need to be protected and/or stewarded more efficiently. This is important work to be done. And for others of us, still, the reinstating or reconfiguring of community politics and community social structures in small and medium-sized towns needs to be addressed and acted upon. Yes, to go home means a lot of work. And maybe it is the work we have been running from all along.

But real progress is often slow. And people, in general, are moving too fast. These observations are emphasized in a short poem in my book *Zoro's Field: My Life in the Appalachian Woods*.

Slow down!/Where are you going in such a rush?/To the supermarket of your last dime?/Is the sound of pencil lead on paper/too much for your ears?/At fifty miles per hour/the butterfly on the rose by the side of the road/is as invisible/as a wish for the answer to prayers./As you run through your best years/watching the road./Faster than the speed of life.

As the places that we remember or live in change dramatically with each passing year, it becomes clearer to me that part of the problem is that those persons who left their original communities for various and sundry "promised lands" never returned with the news and stories of what they saw, experienced and learned. Even though Thomas Wolfe expressed what on the surface seemed to be a disillusionment and distaste for the idea of returning home, it is my deeper belief that what Wolfe was really saying was that he wanted to go home.

With that in mind, what, then, can we imagine might fill the blank pages at the end of Wolfe's book? If I may be so bold as to place myself in his shoes, I would like to suggest that the book's protagonist gives up the adolescent dreams of his youth, reclaims his allegiance to his original mind and his native land, and finds the path that leads him back to the old barns, the laurel slicks and hollers of his youth. Home. Where his body and mind are at rest. Home. Where the trees and the seasons are familiar, like hands. Home. Where winter and summer, rain and snow, are the living hands of the clocks that measure our lives. Home. Where the heart is. Home. Where the work begins.

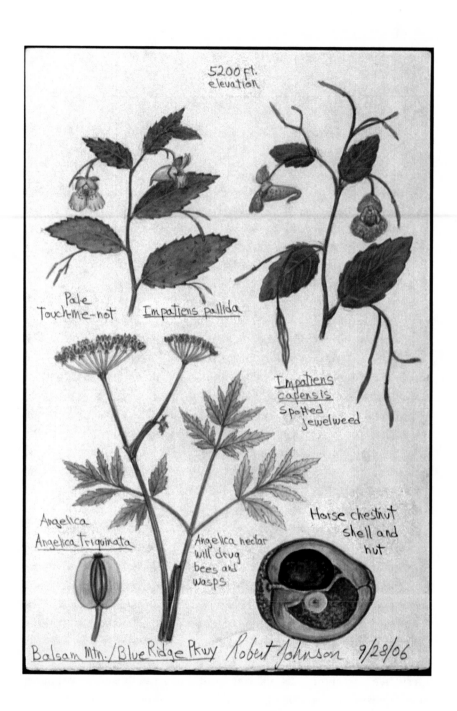

5200 ft.
elevation

Pale
Touch-me-not   Impatiens pallida

Impatiens
capensis
Spotted
Jewelweed

Angelica
Angelica triquinata

Angelica nectar
will drug
bees and
wasps

Horse chestnut
shell and
nut

Balsam Mtn./Blue Ridge Pkwy   Robert Johnson   9/28/06

New Native
Living In Harmony with Place

*People ask where I am from, and I say the confluence of the Sac-
ramento River and San Joaquin River and San Francisco Bay, of
the Alta California Bioregion, of the North Pacific Rim of the Pacific Basin of the Planet Earth.*
> — Peter Berg (founder of Planet Drum) , from a
> talk at the University of North Carolina, 1983

During my itinerant years spent wandering across the U.S., which
lasted into my early thirties, and before I returned to my boyhood
home in western North Carolina, I found myself on the west coast as
part of a northern California community that was working on the ideas
of community and culture by way of creating a new paradigm for
conscious and responsible living called "bioregionalism." For these
folks, bioregionalism meant an escape from the city, a small vegetable
garden, participation in periodic seasonal community ceremonies and
rituals, and an interest and partial adherence to Buddhist and Native
American religion, social ideology and practice.

This bioregional paradigm, which I participated in fully, included,
further, the ideas of reinhabitation, ecological awareness and giving
constitutional rights to non-human species. These ideas and values
were most visibly manifested in the magazine *Planet Drum*, which
permeated much of northern California. These principles could also be
found in creative ventures and/or organizations such as a Reinhabitory
Theatre, a Primitive Arts Institute, and the annual All Species Day
Parade. On the level of social services and community services an
alternative community school was built and an enthusiastic volunteer
Fire Department rejuvenated. All this was based on the perspective that

the well-being of the Earth and the creatures that lived upon it depended upon a human understanding of the importance of biological diversity and man's correct relationship with place. Place as understood in both its microcosmic and macrocosmic realities as they dovetailed with our day-to-day lives and responsibilities towards maintaining a sustainable relationship with the place we call "home."

It is here, at home, that "the real work," as Gary Snyder calls it, begins. And that real work, these days, best begins with the rediscovery of the natural world. And, further, in establishing an intimate relationship with this world. In fact, I would go so far as to say that only in establishing this kind of intimacy will we be able to save ourselves from the on-going and escalating destruction of the natural world.

Most of us have come to be where we live, these days, as uninvited guests. Coming from other places. Coming from other cultures. In many cases (for those of us who have remained or returned to the mountains of western North Carolina and from where I write these words) people who have moved here from outside this region, come here oblivious to and remain unconcerned about that which has culturally preceded them. Oblivious, too, to such things as biology, geology, geography, genealogy and the historical and cultural balances built into these natural and social systems which have coexisted (cohabitated) in relative harmony, if not sustainability, for hundreds, if not thousands, of years.

With the above as background, I would like to offer up the idea of "the new native." By "new native" I mean those persons who have come to live in a place for the first time and feel as if it were home. As "new natives," I would like to suggest that we see ourselves as caretakers of the old, as well as being heralds of the new. And that we come into these new places (in my case, the mountains of western North Carolina) with a sense of reverence, respect and responsibility as if it were our naturally inherent duty that the past be protected, the present enjoyed, and the future assured.

At the core of the body of beliefs that are those of the *new native* there is a belief and an understanding that suggests that what the modern world has given us, has offered up to us as "progress," (and what has now mutated into a concept known as "global capitalism") is not healthy, healing, meaningful or good for either individual or planet. And, further, that all notions of patriarchy and the mega-aggressiveness that is manifested in the accumulation of wealth and power fall back eventually, like sand, into the sea of a repetitively self-destructive history. When living in the embrace of the *new native* paradigm it becomes theoretically possible for extended families to become established as part of our living culture. It becomes possible for new communities to be started, restored, or revived which will survive when economies are based on meaningful work and local produce and where social structures are based on relationships of fraternity and shared commonality rather than economic, racial, and religious demographics. Further, the idea of *new native* advocates a new, more finely-tuned sensitivity to the notion of reinhabitation. It implies an awareness of Jung's notion of the collective unconscious, and the subsequent dream of a possible transfiguration of the human psyche into a new, more spiritual and sense-liberated whole. Hypothetically, this perspective and this way of life produces a total being (a community of total beings) whose values and socio-sexual politics are much more in harmony with the natural psychic-sexual balance of the planet in general, and one's watershed and bioregion, in particular.

As an experiment in bioregional living and living-in-place as a *new native*, I returned to my boyhood home in the Smoky Mountains of North Carolina after a long sojourn that lasted some fifteen years. I returned to live self-sufficiently and alone and in semi-isolation for almost four years in a small cabin amidst several thousand acres of corporate and privately-owned wilderness bordering the Green River in Polk County, North Carolina. This off-the-grid world was very different from today's world of global capitalism, Walmarts, computers, corporate media, and its techno-toys. What I learned from this Thoreau-like experience living in a more natural setting was later taken back out into the greater world and was used to enable me to become involved in projects and organizations such as a project to identify and protect Native American sacred sites in the Southern Appalachians; *Katuah Journal* (a first bioregional journal in the Southeast); the Southern

Biodiversity Project; the Western Carolina Alliance; the Canary Coalition and other pro-preservation groups. This kind of activism came primarily from my experience of living in the wild, but also from my experiences, earlier, on the west coast. In both cases, I brought back what I had learned—to the mountains of my youth as useful ballast and bounty and in the spirit of being able to "go home again," and in doing so, bringing back the news.

Our true cultural ancestors here in North America (and here in the mountains of western North Carolina) are the American Indians. I don't think it's preposterous to suggest that those of us with European geneology have, still, a rather large karmic debt to pay for our less-than-moral exchanges over the past several centuries (which also includes the present day) with the original inhabitants of the Americas. With respect to this would-be debt, I think a good place to begin restitution and settlement would be by implanting a bio-centered ciriculae (along with instruction on the traditional wisdom of native peoples and their knowledge of the natural world) at the center of our existing school systems.

By becoming a *new native* I am not advocating that we all become carbon copies of the Native American of the past, just as I would not advocate that we strive to become the rusty robots of our own science fiction. Being a new native entails, rather, (and without guilt) embracing a consciousness that learns from the ancient cultures that have been here longest and that, therefore, know this place best. With this kind of focused earth-based education, new rituals, celebrations and lifestyles can be conceived of and implemented which are compatible not only with the past, but are more organically modern (and, therefore, more truly progressive) foundations for a more harmonious and sustainable present, and a more hopeful future.

Community
Changing the Good Old Days
into the Good New Ways

What I stand for
Is what I stand on.
— Wendell Berry,
　"Below" in *A Part*

Thinking about my years growing up over in the Smoky Mountains in Graham County, I can remember how isolated it felt and how strong the sense of community was. Winters tended to be more severe than they are now and there were sometimes long stretches of time when folks couldn't get in or out of the little town of Robbinsville, only intensifying the kind of tribal feeling that occurred during times of bad weather. But the community feeling was a warm one, and I remember feeling secure, knowing that in hard times we would take care of one another and that life, somehow, would continue there as it always had.

Those were informative years for me. Years which instilled in my genetic memory something of an idealism where the idea of community was concerned. These memories include those of great congregations of kids gathering at an elder person's home to crack burlap sacks full of walnuts, or neighborhood work days to help someone pick tobacco or build or repair a barn. I was just a boy and so hadn't experienced, first hand, the kinds of antagonistic things that adults can do to each other in terms of disturbing or even destroying community relations. The idea of "community" has stayed with me through the years, and even though I am, by nature, a solitary sort, in my more vulnerable and insecure moments, I long for those youthful days in Robbinsville and that front-porch, extended family kind of life.

As the saying goes, those were the good old days. Days long gone. Even in small towns like the one in which I now live in Jackson County, not far from where I grew up, the word "community" is rarely used. Old buildings that have served as community centers and general stores are used sparingly, are in disrepair, or are completely gone. All the roads have been paved (by a North Carolina legislative mandate) and old Highway 281 which runs in front of my one-hundred-and-thirty-year-old country farmhouse is busy with continuous traffic both night and day. These days one is more likely to catch up on news or local gossip from neighbors in the housewares section of the new Super Walmart than at a community center pot luck or from friends casually dropping in. Life in the fast lane, it seems, has come to Tuckasegee.

The *American Heritage Dictionary of the English Language* defines *community* as "a group of plants and animals living in a specific region under relatively similar conditions; ecology; fellowship." This definition is a good place to start, as here the idea of community does not only imply human life, but rather that of all plants and animals—using the terms "ecology" to put things in a more holistic and therefore proper perspective. Here, interdependent intercourse and interaction are implied, as is the notion of stewardship and education. In the "good old days," both of these probably would have been considered essential to the well-being of the community. And one should not forget the "fellowship" in the dictionary definition, which in days gone by was a continuous and daily conversation with those whose paths would cross in the local barbershop, the feed store, or the general store as the years and generation passed by. These days, folks, even in the country, barely know their neighbors. They are more likely to spend any free time with TV sit-com families than their own—more likely to spend more time on the Internet "chatting" than in actual conversation with folks from down the road. Times have changed. Things are not as I remember them growing up in Milltown along Snowbird Creek.

In his book *The Geography of Nowhere*, James Kunstler talks about the loss of community:

> Community is not something you have, like pizza. Nor is it something you can buy, as visitors to Disneyland and Williamsburg discover. It is a living organis m based on a web of interdependencies—which is to say, a local economy. It expresses itself physically as connectedness, as buildings actively relating to one another, and to whatever public space exists, be it the street, or the courthouse square, or the village green. "Most important," Wendell Berry writes, "it must be generally loved and competently cared for by its people, who, individually, identify their own interest with the interest of their neighbors." This notion of community began to vanish in America after World War II. Our small towns have never been worse off than they are now.

No short paragraph that I've ever read on the subject of *community* hits the heart of this issue deeper than this.

It seems that everywhere I look these days pertaining to the subject of *community*, I run across the ideas of "fellowship" and "sustainable economy." As our communities have broken down, and been replaced with various and sundry technologies and box stores, the skills which have fostered neighborliness have been lost in just a single generation. It would seem that, today, community has more to do with consumerism than conservation and what we share in common.

In his seminal book on global cultures and ecology, *The Great Work*, Thomas Berry has this to say on the subject of *community*: "We have lost immense areas of intimate knowledge carried in traditional craft and in farming skills, knowledge that provides a relationship between the human community and the natural world that is immensely more bountiful and less destructive than that of large-scale business projects. The well-being of each component part [of the community] is intimately related to the well-being of the other parts and to the well-being of the whole."

On this common sense note, Berry continues his soliloquy by expanding the vision of what *community* ultimately entails. "Every mode of being has inherent rights to their place in the single community that is the Earth community. Rights that come by existence itself. The intimacy of humans with the other components of the planet is the fulfillment of each in the other and all within the single Earth community. It is a spiritual fulfillment as well as a mutual support. It is a commitment, not simply a way of survival." These were sentiments, I admit, that were only consciously understood by me around the age of thirty—during the years when I lived alone in the woods of Polk County, where my community included as much, and maybe more, the plant and animal life as it did the human. But even then, we were all dependent upon one another (with the plants and animals less dependent upon me than I upon them) and lived in close proximity with necessary and mutual respect.

So, how, then, you might ask, are we to go about restoring *community* and community values to our towns, our lives? People like James Kunstler say that we are entering an era when small towns will be valued again, and that out of necessity we will reinvent truly social economies using local assets and resources. Should this happen, it would seem inevitable that community sentiments and values would be, gradually, restored.

While it's all too true that we can't go back to "the good old days," we can move forward to "the good new ways." This hypothetical shift can include some of the more essential and traditional aspects of the good old days at a juncture when solitary independence is being replaced by the notion and practice of interdependence. In these kinds of communities where local governments might have a greater degree of autonomy than they do now, and where monies are circulated and recycled more amongst their own population, this revenue can be more equananimously filtered back into local funding recepticals to benefit those with less or with greater needs. (Remember "community chests"?). I'm envisioning a community where each member has a place and finds appropriate and meaningful work based on the self-realized merits of his or her own strengths and weaknesses rather than through affiliations with party politics or social class. In this model, where barter is accepted and even encouraged, work is generated, allowing community members to stay at home rather than "work off." I see this kind of community as self-perpetuating, becoming increasingly stronger from generation to generation as new people are incorporated into the community from the outside and their offspring's lives take on meaning by simply being a part of such a greater recognizable and responsible community which also acts as a social and psychological mirror for any acts of generosity or bad behavior generated by the young. Such a community becomes a place of "continuous harmony" as Wendell Berry calls it. A kind of harmony that functions simply. We are all neighbors in this simple paradigm. Growing. Separately. To-gether.

Let me end by saying that I have always liked the sentiments es-poused in Occam's Razor—that the simplest and most direct way to do anything is always the best. This implies, inherently, the adage that "small is beautiful." The beauty of sustainable community is that, for the most part, it is about simplicity and human-scale eco-dynamics. It is a small paradigm. And small, as far as I can see, is the only way that works.

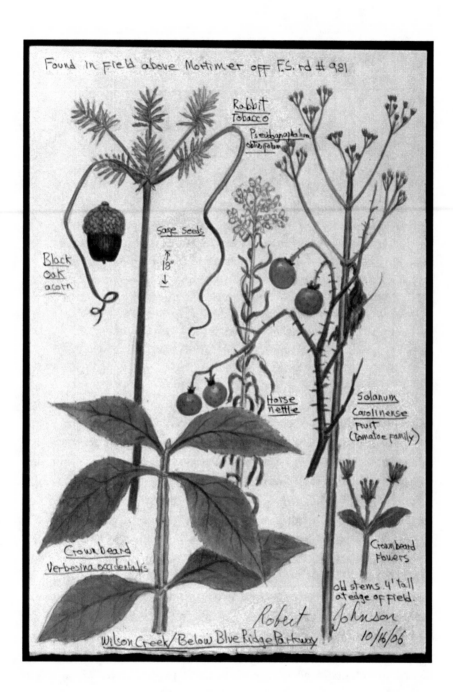

Found in Field above Mortimer off F.S. rd # 981

Rabbit Tobacco
Pseudognaphalium obtusifolium

Black Oak acorn

Sage Seeds
↑
18"
↓

Horse nettle

Solanum Carolinense Fruit (Tomatoe family)

Crownbeard Flowers

Crownbeard
Verbesina occidentalis

old stems 4' tall at edge of field.

Robert Johnson
10/16/06

Wilson Creek / Below Blue Ridge Parkway

29

What is Sacred

The Spirit in Place
(Sacred Sites in the Southern Appalachians)

. . . before the coming of Christianity all the peoples of the Old World had lived in a numinous landscape spangled with sacred markers and sacred places. The land itself was believed to be alive and under the protection of numina, guardian spirits. In such a world one did not blithely cut down a grove of trees, plow up virgin meadowland, dam a stream or divert it. An alteration of the landscape had to be carefully couched in propitiatory rituals. Intended to appease the numina.
— Frederick Turner, *Spirit of Place: The Making of an American Landscape*

In the 1980s, while working as director for a project to identify and protect Native American sacred sites in the Southern Appalachians, my cohorts and I, while trying to do educational and activist work pertaining to this project, faced considerable opposition from big land owners and self-serving local government officials. This took the form of everything from slanderous attacks and character assassinations in local and regional newspapers to, in one case, death threats. My loosely-knit team of traditional Cherokee elders, folklorists, archeologists and volunteers from both the Native American and Anglo communities were fighting what was definitely an uphill battle, if not an escalating war. But we persisted—at least long enough to see sanctions written into the National Forest Service "Fifty-Year Plan" which included mandatory consultation with Cherokee officials before logging or making roads on Forest Service land. These regulations were designed to safeguard and protect any to-be-logged areas which might include sites of religious or historical importance.

During these years and this work, we experienced something of a revival with regards to the white, European interest in things "native," and specifically with regard to people of this region and their ethnological heritage. Here in western North Carolina as soon as it became ok, or "cool" to admit to Indian blood lines in their family lineage, I began getting phone calls, letters and faxes on almost a daily basis. I got calls from people asking about certain places that might have religious or historical significance in their area or on their land. I got calls asking for more information as to where to go to get in-depth genealogical counseling. All kinds of questions. All kinds of stories and family history. We had, quite literally, opened a genealogical and cultural Pandora's Box. While there was, on the one hand, a war going on between the Project directors and the powers-that-be, there was also, simultaneously, an ethnological renaissance of sorts occurring in the population of western North Carolina at large. It seemed at the time as if some kind of acceptance was beginning to replace generations of denial. Interest was replacing apathy.

Today, following a major blood-degree controversy, the ousting of a Principal Chief on grounds of corruption, the institution of a strong traditional activist organization, and the building of the Harrah's Cherokee Casino, things are very different over on the Qualla Boundary. For the first time in what some would say has been a long, long time, there are many more obvious and public signs that the traditional life would truly seem to be alive and well. While during the reign of Robert Youngdeer as Principal Chief, the official policy on traditional matters involving the tribe was, "The Cherokee no longer practice the old traditional ways," today the tribe has a recognized traditional spokesman in the person of elder Walker Calhoun. A reinvigorated Cherokee Language Program is being promoted by the Tribal Council with a focus on the very young members of the tribe in order to keep the language and the traditional culture from going extinct. The old ways are becoming part of the new ways and a more appropriate balance is being reached. The idea as to what is sacred is changing, as all things do and should.

At the same time, things are changing out in the world of the dominant culture, as the population demographics for western North Carolina are becoming more diverse with the influx from outside the region of new first and second home residents. Many of these "furiners," as the locals refer to them, are bringing with them certain ecological values and attitudes from their former lives and places of residence. This influx and these outsider values have made a significant impact on eco-activism in western North Carolina, as seen in the growth in size and influence of any number of conservation/ecology organizations. With all the press and with all the controversy surrounding certain pressing environmental issues in this region, the question of the sacredness of the natural world has been raised, over and over, again and again.

North Carolina native and ecologian Thomas Berry has written in his 1999 landmark publication *The Great Work*, "In the end, it is the land that is the most sacred element of our lives." This statement is not some kind of new age or hippie heresy. To my way of thinking, this is just plain good common sense. If we don't hold the earth and all its life forms as sacred, as worthy of a certain sense of reverence and equanimity, then we are, in a very direct way, undermining our own welfare and well-being. For, without a healthy environment, we, as humans, cannot hope to live any semblance of a healthy life. One thing predetermines the other. Without the essentials of clean air and clear water, all other systems are irrelevant.

In the eighties when we were working on the Sacred Sites Project, I got to witness, first hand, not only traditional ceremony, but was able to spend time in (sacred) places that were truly special in that they exuded a numinous energy or exhibited a personality of presiding divinity that was not only physically noticeable but was remarkable. There was a consistency, I noted, in where these kinds of places were found. Geographically, there were waterfalls, groves of trees, springs, mountain peaks, rock cliffs—characteristics that when chanced upon in the course of normal daily travel gave me pause to slow down, pay attention, and take note.

As I became more and more enamored of these "special" places, I was taken aside one day by one of our project elders and given a real talking to. "All places are sacred," he said. "All equally, and should be treated as such. The idea that one place is more sacred than another is foreign to our Cherokee beliefs. Everything is sacred. To divide and separate one thing from another is a white man's concept. We believe that everything is inter-related and part of a larger web of life."

Ultimately, I found myself wondering what the implications are for this kind of thinking, for all of us today? If we embrace these kinds of ideas, I often think to myself, then how can we justify any emotion other than horror concerning such recent regional travesties as the toxification of the Barber Orchards land in Haywood County, the pollution of the Pidgeon River by the paper industry, the pollution of the air in and around the Great Smokies from coal-fueled power plants, the practice of clear-cutting as regulated by the Forest Service, and for that matter any human activity that is carried out in the natural world (that includes, also, our towns and cities) without reverence and re-spect, without a thought to the future and the well-being of future generations.

What is sacred? In a very real sense, and as the traditional peoples have believed for thousands of years the Earth itself is a sacred temple, a church, a gift and a covenant from God. (In her work as Western Carolina University archeologist, Ann Rogers has recently carbon-dated an Indian inhabitation site here in the mountains at 10,000 years!) Would we dare to swear in or desecrate a church? If not, why would we want to be any less respectful towards the Earth itself—which literally gives us sustenance and life, and without which we could not and would not exist.

When I am in my garden, here, next to the Tuckaseigee River, I try to work with a sense of well-being and reverence—for the rich soil and the relatively clean water nearby. I grow my crops organically and without any easy poisons. I do this out of respect for myself and for my family and for the continued well-being of the land—that others, after me, may benefit, too, from a healthy soil. That they might benefit from my labors by inheriting a place from which they, too, may harvest healthy food.

Many years have gone by, and I am middle-aged. Only now am I truly beginning to replace my European values (with so much emphasis placed on the separation and isolation of things) with those of my traditional Cherokee neighbors—who see things in a much more holistic way. But I'm making progress. My Cherokee friends make fun of me and tease me. "You'll get it, someday," they say, laughing. But I know I've still got a long way to go, as I work diligently to better see the bigger picture that comes so easily to my Indian friends. A picture in which there is a world where we are all related and where *everything* is sacred.

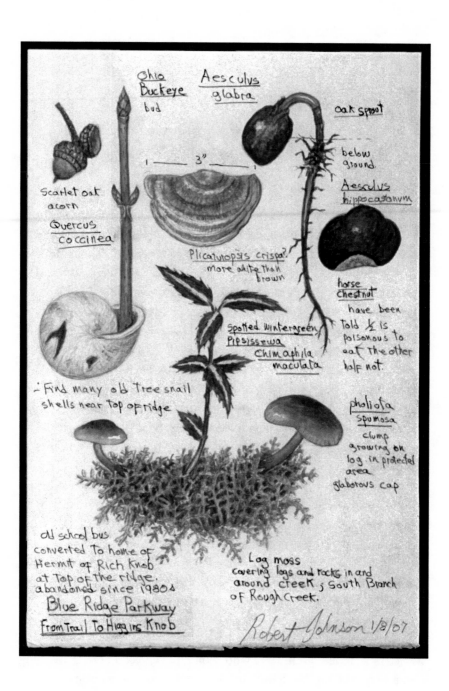

Ohio Buckeye bud — Aesculus glabra

oak sproot

below ground

Aesculus hippocastanum

Scarlet oak acorn
Quercus coccinea

| 3" |

Plicaturopsis crispa? more white than brown

horse chestnut have been told ½ is poisonous to eat the other half not.

Spotted wintergreen Pipsissewa Chimaphila maculata

- Find many old tree snail shells near top of ridge

pholiota spumosa clump growing on log in protected area glaborous cap

old school bus converted to home of Hermit of Rich Knob at top of the ridge, abandoned since 1980s
Blue Ridge Parkway
From Trail To Higgins Knob

Log moss covering logs and rocks in and around creek; South Branch of Rough Creek.

Robert Johnson 1/8/07

35

Overpopulation
Carrying Capacity For Western
North Carolina & The World

When I returned to western North Carolina in 1978 after being gone for more than fifteen years, on the surface things looked about the same as they did when I had left. With the exception of a few new interstate roads, the countryside, the towns, the rivers, the wilderness seemed to be pretty much intact. The clean air and the clean water and the thousands of acres of unspoiled wilderness that I had enjoyed as a boy growing up in Graham County and that had brought me back home, at first glance seemed to have survived. I reveled in this misperception for almost four years while I lived wild and self-sufficiently over in Polk County not far from the Green River Gorge. But in 1984, after emerging Rip Van Winkle-like from my Spartan, made-from-Thoreau lair and moving to Jackson County to a piece of land I had bought in the Caney Fork watershed, I began to sense, in fact to see, "the change."

"I'm holding on to most of my land here in Jackson County," said Eugene Brown as I signed the papers for the deed to my land. "I'm holding out for the big boom that's coming. It won't be long before Jackson County will be discovered by the same people who are moving into Cashiers and Highlands. They've got the big money and that money's gonna make it's way down the mountain into Sylva and Cullowhee, I'm certain of that." At the time, I remember thinking that Mr. Brown had gone a little mad with his dreams of the Florida and New York money making its way into quiet, uneventful Cullowhee and Sylva. As it turned out it was I who should have been in therapy coping with a very real case of denial, if not in school taking a basic course in economics, maybe coupled with a crash course in "Wilderness

Naiveté." Sure enough, all along what was once an old dirt logging road leading to my land, there are now Florida summer homes and dug foundations, just as there are all up and down John's Creek Road. Mr. Brown, it turns out, has become a real estate prophet, as many of his predictions have come true.

Twenty years have come and gone since my curious conversation with Mr. Brown. In that time one could reasonably say that "all hell has broken loose" here in western North Carolina in the form of a population and development explosion that is as Armageddon-like (to those of us who moved back here to escape the urbanization and suburbanization of America) as were St. John of Patmos's predictions to the millennial-mad Y2Kers. These days everywhere you look along the mountain faces and ridges, along the rivers, in pastures and old farm land, there are trailers moving in or McMansions going up. Just down the road, the Great Smokies National Park is the most visited recreation area in the country. Almost all our major rivers are bordered by white water businesses. And the unkindest cut of all may be the recent figures from the National Climactic Center giving the mountains of western North Carolina one of the worst pollution ratings in the entire country. Armageddon, indeed!

A good case-in-point to the kind of "growth" and "development" we are talking about would be the "strip" in Sylva. The shy, quiet little mountain town of Sylva has become a mini-metropolis, with a strip of fast-food and convenience businesses lining both sides of the road in both directions out of town for four or five miles and reminiscent of what one would expect to find in Los Angeles rather than here in the feet of the Appalachians in the mountain South.

With no measurable increase in new industry in the area, I can't for the life of me figure out where the people are coming from—that patronize the small businesses that have taken over old Highway 107. At this point, the explosion of small (and large if we figure in the overnight appearances of a super Walmart and a Lowe's superstore) businesses would seem to greatly exceed even the exponential increase in building of second homes that are fast filling up the counties' accessible (and inaccessible) land. Where are the people coming from?!

Clearly, with the strip-mall businesses and Walmart booming, the people who patronize them are here. Clearly, the remote, "back-woods" Jackson County I knew as a boy and more recently as a mid-aged land owner, is gone. What has replaced all this is a tidal wave of "American progress" stemming from a decade of a booming economy. But more importantly, what has happened here in Jackson County, as it has all over western North Carolina, is the advent of *overpopulation.*

In 1994, when I first became aware of the actual statistics of the global population explosion, I wrote the following paragraph:

> What we are hearing on the nightly news from our politicians, from our educators, from our "experts" concerning the current disruptive state of the world, are only the peripheral symptoms, the residual camouflage of a greater nemesis: overpopulation. At the end of the millennial root of all our social, cultural, medical, psychological and pathological ills is the fact that the Earth is too crowded. There are too many people and not enough space, not enough food, not enough money, not enough (clean) air, not enough organized wisdom to approach any sort of human balance whereas the environment and our individual lives are concerned. In conversation or in public debate the subject of *overpopulation* is always avoided. Never addressed. In order to even attempt setting things back into at state of balance on a regional or global scale, the true cause of all our problems needs to be addressed. Space is running out, as is time, and the issue of whether or not we will learn to recognize and curtail our indulgences before we infest the entire planet like a plague of locusts, needs attention now. By everyone.

While, world-wide, the human population is growing at the rate of more than 300,000 people a day, 100 million a year, with the average yearly global household income predicted to fall from $18,000 to $800 in the next twenty five years, and with the average number of children born to procreating females at 5.5, with less than 10% of married couples using birth control, and the total population of the planet expected to reach 10 billion by the end of the present decade, does it not follow that at least some of this escalating wave of humanity should be spilling over on to the "shores" of the Southern Appalachians? Where are they coming from? They are coming from everywhere! If I've got my numbers right, then things are even bleaker than I wanted to believe. If these numbers are correct, there's no more time for denial or naïve ignorance. The facts and the bodies are here! Right in front of us. Along our roads and mountaintops.

The implications of this explosion are clear, if not obvious: the more people there are the less there is for everyone. (And by everyone I also include all plant and animal wildlife.) Less land. Less food. Less (clean) air and clean water. Fewer farms. Fewer jobs, less meaningful work, and not nearly as much quiet. And with "the less," there is also "the more": more noise, more pollution, more crowding, more traffic, more taxes, more corruption, more illness (including mental illness). The bottom line here is what is referred to these days in the environmental movement vernacular as "carrying capacity." *Carrying capacity* is the measure of how much or how little balance a particular ecosystem or environmental community has or has not. With its burgeoning population there is simply not enough carrying capacity for our bioregion to support such an influx of humanity on so small and rugged an area. Our mountain ecosystem and its myriad parts simply cannot "carry" the load of humanity it is being asked to support. In short, after a certain point there's just not enough of everything to go around.

When a human is ill, there are symptoms (fever, fatigue, nausea, weakness, paleness of skin) and we seek a physician—someone who is trained to help us put our bodies back into a state of balance and health. When the environment is out of sorts, we also see symptoms—change in weather conditions, wider foraging ranges for predatory animals, smaller game populations for human consumption, substantial decrease in animal and plant species, polluted air and water, an increase in erratic or anti-social behavior in animals and humans, pandemic disease. To whom do we go to cure these kinds of ills? Who and where are the "dirt doctors?" The best answer to this question may be that they are us—all of us.

When I read the local newspapers and magazines these days, it's like reading about developing countries on the other side of the planet. Waynesville, just down the road, has an EPA Superfund cleanup site. The pollution index in the Smokies is off the graph. The evergreens are dying off by the thousands at the higher elevations on the Blue Ridge Parkway and on Mt. Mitchell. Ponds and lakes are testing high for air-born particulates and pollutants. The crime rates are higher than ever. Small businesses are going under due to the incursion of mega-corporations and their box-stores. Wildlife populations and habitat are on a serious decline. And the list goes on....

A daunting list, this. So what are we to do? One thing is clear, that on the way toward achieving a sustainable balance and achieving a manageable *carrying capacity*, there is much work to be done in terms of building bridges between human and non-human life forms both here in the Smokies and world-wide. Life forms that are important, even essential, to our very survival. Life forms that need to be allowed to stay healthy and survive if we human are going to remain healthy and alive. In order to achieve this kind of stasis, certain limits must be imposed on so-called "progress" and "development." This, of course, will be very unpopular during such economically and technologically "high times." The burden of this challenge is on all of us—to recognize and admit that we are failing in our attempts to solve big problems with little solutions. We need, instead, to begin initiating creative macro-phase solutions to our macro-phase problems.

In the end, I agree with the sentiments of Thomas Berry when he says that we must become, again as we once were, more intimate with our natural surrounding and begin relating to the Earth as an object rather than a subject, or something to be possessed and conquered. If we can do this, Berry says, then we may also stand a chance of restoring (or at least reinventing) the kind of harmony and balance necessary to live a full, rich life. By embracing this kind of awareness and sense of stewardship, the burden of overpopulation can, over time, be brought under control. Realistically, it will probably mean instituting legislation that imposes regulations on the numbers of people that can inhabit any given area of land. Laws governing the number of children a family can have, with appropriate prevention-induced fines for non-compliance.

I have, by now, had to sell my four acres over in the Caney Fork watershed. For the last fifteen years I've been living in an old farm-house along the Tuckaseigee River that was built in the 1890s. The question I am asking myself these days is: How much longer will this old farm, surrounded as it is by pastures, woods and the Tuckaseigee River, and populated by all kinds of wildlife and native plants, remain the way it is? How long before these old overgrown pastures full of foxes, wild turkey and bobcats will be over-run with trailers, or even worse: condominiums and gated communities? How long before the natural quietude and the sound of birdsong I so enjoy is transmogrified into human and machine-made noise? Some may shrug off such questions in apathetic indifference, saying "Oh well, time will tell." But, sadly, time is what we, now, have so little of.

Water as Archetype and Sacred Font

Dedicated to Sam Gray
May 5, 1939 – August 18, 2005

The force that drives the water through the rocks
Drives my red blood.
                                        — Dylan Thomas

As a boy growing up in and around the high-elevation coniferous temperate rainforests of the Great Smoky Mountains of western North Carolina, I loved the rain. Especially the daily summer storms that, Zeus-like, rose up from behind the mountains in the afternoon, appearing without warning with fireworks of thunder and lightning and a deluge of water.

Water has always, it seems, been a part of my life's dharma, just as it has graced every landscape in which I have lived. The creeks and branches of my boyhood. The oceans of my youthful manhood. The rivers of my middle age. "God-willin' and the creek don't rise" is a favorite idiomatic expression here in the mountain South. Well, God must be willin', 'cause the creek (in actuality, the Tuckaseigee River) across the road from my house has been rising a lot lately! Living in the flood plain and a hundred yards from the river, it seems as if every time it rains I am evacuated. Volunteer firemen, in the middle of the night, knocking on my door. Being downstream from a series of four successive TVA dams, there is always the chance of a catastrophe. My emergency bags are always packed. Water is always a part of this landscape—whether it is real or fearfully imagined.

In 1988, with the little bit of money I received from a structured insurance settlement following a debilitating car accident that happened during a snow storm, and not having enough capital to buy or build a house, I embarked upon a project to build a tower. A tower built in the archetypal tradition of Carl Jung, Robinson Jeffers, William Butler Yeats, James Joyce, Montaigne, Holderlin, Rilke and Frank Lloyd Wright. A spire. A steeple from which to write. On a small, remotely located four-acre lot I had bought with the first installment of the insurance money a few years earlier, I visualized, drew, and broke ground for the tower. "Springhouse" I would call it, since the spot where I decided to construct the three-story, octagon-shaped structure was situated right next to the head of a free-flowing spring. In fact, I would learn from a local dowser whom I had enticed to dowse the property, I was building on what he called "a water-dome." On this piece of property which I had bought because of its abiding solemnity that invoked the sacred, water was the principal identifying feature. An elemental personality that also exuded a tangible, yet universal, sense of calm that resembled something like sleep.

Later, I would learn from my near neighbors that my spring was considered to be somewhat sacred among members of the community. They conjured up stories told to them by their parents and grandparents, some going back in reference to days prior to the settlement of the Europeans in these mountains and that involved the spring and the high regard in which it was held. My friend and neighbor in the Webster community, Sam Gray, whose people had migrated into the Caney Fork community from Polk and McDowell counties where they had settled generations before, was, at the time, working as Museum Curator at the Mountain Heritage Center in Cullowhee and was working on a "water" project for an exhibition. Tangentially, and as a piece to be contributed to one of the early issues of *Katuah Journal: A Bioregional Journal for the Southern Appalachians,* Sam wrote the following poem, entitled "Water Drum," which he said attempted to touch on the traditional as well as the archetypal aspects of water.

> *We begin somewhere in water*
> *As does everything*

A water drum beats within us
And within all things
Drumming the falling waters and rain
Interuterine, the first language
Was water. An arc of water
Translates the promise of God
And the sun into colors
Drawn from every mind
The black waters of history
Mingle the lambent waters of time
While a water drum calls within us
That like heaven and earth
We are mostly the wanderings of water...
That without this, and love, we
Dry up and blow away.

My contacts over the years with Cherokees on both the Qualla and the Snowbird Boundaries had led me, prior to buying my land, to a Cherokee elder and medicine person, who gave me the following discourse on the subject of the sacredness of water.

We have been told that the river is "yunwi gunahita": The Long Human Being. It is called so because it is alive—alive just as we are.

We have been told that if you do not believe this: then go to the water and do not drink. If you do not drink, you will die. Water is the Life-Giver. If water were not alive, how could it give us life?

Because water is a living being, we were told, we do not spit in water, urinate in water, defecate in water, or vomit in water. We respect the water as we would respect an elder of our own people.

We have been told that the water talks. Go to a waterfall. Fast and pray and listen. If you go there with an open heart, we are told, sometimes the water will speak in such a way as you might understand. It is then that the water will speak of wonderful things. For the water is always talking. And to hear its voice we need only to prepare ourselves in silence, and wait...

We have been told that the function of water is: flowing. Flowing brings cleansing, change, purification, and healing. Water manifests as a great power upon the Earth. Springs rise up from the Underworld, which is known as the place of spirits. Water brings that spirit power, up, and into this world. The branches, creeks, streams, and rivers carry, then, this power to all the parts of the world. So, we go to the water to drink of that spirit power.

Water also rises from the Underworld of our own subconscious being, we were told. If we do not plunge into the inner parts of ourselves and explore the deepest pools within, the waters of destiny rise until the dams of our carefully constructed and protected identity are burst in a flood of elemental power which is expressed through the tributaries of our anger, passion, violence, tenderness and fear.

We have been told that the most balanced way to be is found by following the trail of the natural forces within and around ourselves. And this, too, is the way of water.

We were told that if in need of healing or purification, to go to water. To go to the creek or to the river, they told us, and shed your clothes as if they were nothing more than old skin. And standing in that sacred place where the shallow water touches the bank, offer gratitude and thanks to the water in the form of prayer.

We were told to then plunge underwater seven times, giving thanks to the water with each plunge. And in this manner, healing will come.

We were told to release and let go of all old thoughts. Of all old desires. And to let the imperfections float away from us, downstream, with all other debris that may be floating by. Now, open all your pores and senses to the water, they told us. Let the water enter your soul like you would a lover. And in this way the needed and desired strength will come.

We have been told that men need to go to the water on the new moon of each month. Just as the womanbody is purified each month, so, too, do men need to go to water to be cleansed and renewed.

We were told that it sometimes takes courage to plunge into cold water. Entering cold water is like facing our own death, we were told. When we enter another world, and our identity is lost to the swirling newness and abruptness of the unusual and the unknown... And it is then that we can experience rebirth. And emerging from the womb of our own dying, we are new-born. And the world is seen with young and clear-born eyes, as it is.

I began actual work on the construction of the tower by digging deep holes in which to set the piers or posts which would support the structure. In the first hole I dug, about a foot or so down, I struck water. And in each successive hole: water again! A water-dome, just like the old dowser had said.

Now, I was faced with the dilemma of building a substantial structure that would essentially be sitting in water. And running water, at that. Before I decided to abandon the chosen site, I consulted with a local builder-friend who lived a couple ridges over from the land where I was beginning to build the tower. Tom West, an imaginative and experienced builder, took the time to show me how to cover the 6" x 6" piers in creosote, how to line the holes with gravel, and to pour the concrete—just so—in order that the wooden piers would be secure and the durability of the piers in a watery base would be insured. The bottom line was that treated and creosoted posts sitting in moving water would actually harden over time. Petrify to some extent. This bit of knowledge I had, of course, never heard. A revelation of sorts, it allowed me to go ahead with my plans to build the tower on the spring site, as I had desired.

While building the tower it snowed, rained, and on some mornings I was socked in with fog. Other times I was brought to tears by the beauty of the wood and glass building, the graceful lines of the second-floor ceiling accentuated by large sculpted redwood rafters, and the large windows that looked out into the woods. In the end, not only was the tower a beautiful building, but it looked and felt very much part of the place. It fit the landscape as if it had risen organically from the soil—like a morel mushroom or the mystical appearance of Indian pipes after an early spring rain. For me, in its finished form, Springhouse was a sacred space. It had been built with a heavy dose of *gnosis*, but also with a good bit of *eros*. Clearly, this was a poet's place. And immediately I was reminded of a poem by the Asheville poet Jeff Davis from a series of water-based poems he had been writing for some time on the subject of the native mountain rhododendron. Here, water is also the messenger of love.

Green River

There must be
water to open the earth
To the digging root, to ease its entry
deeper.

Here, it wore the land
hollow.
Low willows
watch water slip
over stones
through thick

rhododendron,
tree-rose, kalmia,
laurel wood.

This was your river,
Lady of the Rivers,
when I came to you lost
in my own thicket of
mind's perplexity,
and you bathed me
in the torpor of a vivid sleep,
anointed me, joined me
to the body of the land
your river passed through,
took me beyond
myself, and the argument
I let die as it mingled
with the cool air, lost
among the leaves.

And still
The water that she was remains
to find its way always
down through the scattered
stones of her forgotten
sanctuary,
creek to river,
to ocean, there raised
up to spirit once more, into
the moving ether, to fall
on these hills as rain,
opening the soil,
sustaining by her stream
the oaks, the rose tree,
lichens, moss, and all below.

Floating in water, as it was, I would think of the tower as a kind of ship as I sat up in the second floor in front of the large windows and looking out into the rhododendron-sea of the surrounding woods. As the helmsman of my "ship," the land around me felt oceanic. Wave-like. Rolling. As captain of my wooden ship, I experienced the tower as not only a place of refuge away from the madding crowds, but a place for solitude, contemplation, and of journey. With the sound of the spring rippling over small stones just outside the open downstairs windows acting as a kind of seductive sedative, daydreams were never far away.

In addition to simply enjoying the serenity and poetic ambience of the place, I also used the water on the property for practical and even metaphysical purposes. The water coming from the main springhead beside the tower I found to be not only some of the most delicious water I've ever drunk in the wild, but filled with so much abundant mineral content that it seems to have certain healing properties. As a result, I found myself going to Springhouse and the spring when in need of physical, mental or emotional medicine. In almost every case, I found relief, if not healing, from the spring water. Sometimes the water was ingested, taken internally, and sometimes it was used ceremonially in more exterior ritualistic fashion. In every individual case there was relief. I don't question this phenomenon. Nor am I surprised by it. Like people are who and what they are, this place is the way it is. Full of the kind of personality as would be anyone with water signs prevalent in their astrological chart.

As I write this, the words from George Harrison's song "Pisces Fish" from his posthumous CD come to mind: "I'm a Pisces fish and the river runs through my soul." When spending time at Springhouse, no matter what I am doing, whether it be outdoor or indoor work or indoor or outdoor relaxation, I'm always aware of a river running through my soul. Water. It's always present. Always there. We are blessed with a plentiful amount of water in these mountains—in our weather, our springs, and our rivers. May it continue.

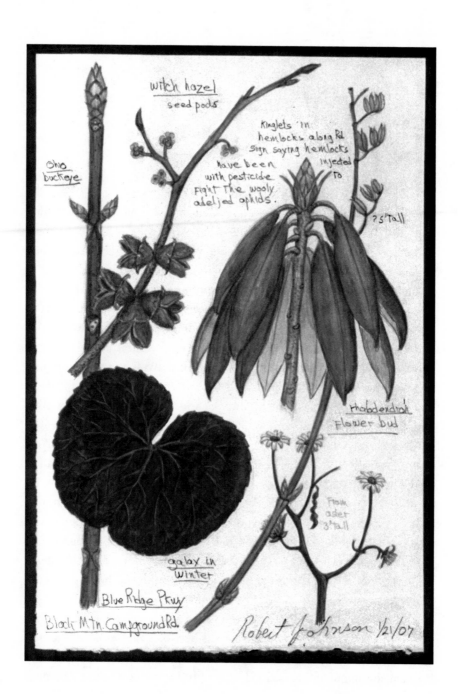

witch hazel
seed pods

Ohio
buckeye

Kinglets in
hemlocks along Rd.
Sign saying hemlocks
have been injected
with pesticide
Fight The wooly
adelied aphids.

?5'Tall

rhododendron
Flower bud

From
aster
3'tall

galax in
winter

Blue Ridge Pkwy
Black Mtn. Campground Rd.

Robert Johnson 1/21/07

51

Cold Mountain
The Book and the Place

The road to Cold Mountain starting from where I live along the Tuckaseigee River in the Canada community of Jackson County, goes up, over and across the Blue Ridge Parkway at Devil's Courthouse and down the other side following the Bubbling Springs Branch headwaters into the Pigeon River watershed along the west fork. On a brilliantly clear day in early fall, after having just finished Charles Frazier's best-selling novel, *Cold Mountain*, Nan Watkins and I got in my pickup truck and set off to see for ourselves the place where this extraordinary first novel was set—some one hundred and fifty years ago—in Haywood County and to explore it as well as to visually and mentally record the similarities and the differences between Frazier's Civil War era Great Balsam Mountains and the greater Southern Blue Ridge Mountains of today.

This book, which spent the better part of 1997 as #1 on *the New York Times Review of Books* Bestseller List, captured the imagination of the nation, if not took it by storm. And for a first-book author with local ties, this is remarkable, if not a first. So, when Nan and I jumped in my truck to go over to Haywood County and the area Frazier writes so eloquently about in his book, I halfway expected to find bumper to bumper traffic along Route 215—with sightseers all waiting to get a firsthand look at, or photo of, the characters from the book emerging out of the past from present-day ramshackled mountain homes.

As we reached the plateau of the Parkway along 215 and made our way into the Cold Mountain watershed between Lickstone Ridge and Fork Mountain, the fall leaves there were just reaching their peaks— brilliant, luminous golds defined strikingly in contrast against the dark forest greens of the high mountain firs and pines.

In Frazier's novel we get detailed and intimate glimpses into a world of such seeming ancient history it almost reads like myth. Or maybe this is just credit to Frazier's mature eye and his deftness at telling a tale. In any case, the seasons, the towns, roads and woodlands leap off the pages of *Cold Mountain*, surrounding us, putting us there.

> The window was tall as a door, and he had imagined many times that it would open onto some other place and let him walk through and be there. Childhood places. The damp creek bed where Indian pipes grew. The corner of a meadow favored by brown-and-black caterpillars in the fall. A hickory limb that overhung the land, and from which he often watched his father driving cows down to the barn at dusk. They would pass underneath him, and in the dirt grew fainter and fainter until it vanished into the calls of katydids and peepers. The window apparently wanted only to take his thoughts back. Which was fine with him, for he had seen the metal face of the age and had been so stunned by it that when he thought into the future, all he could vision was a world from which everything he counted important had been banished or had willingly fled.

As we made our way winding down the descent of the Bubbling Springs road following the stream through the Sunburst community and into the recently man-made Lake Logan area of the Pisgah National Forest, and with the sun at it zenith in the mid-day sky, I was struck with the starkness and solemnity of the place, with the shadows of the north-facing ridges casting long cold glances over the tightly adjacent and steep, sloping hills facing south. And even in brilliant sunshine the valley which housed the imagined 19th century town of Cold Mountain in Frazier's book, was a place that seemed to defy habitation. A place bleak, damp, cold. Hence the name "Cold" mountain, I thought to myself. But in its shadowy tight-ridged bleakness, the current-day Cold Mountain landscape seemed to perfectly mirror the picture of a tough survivalist lifestyle and marauding bands of Home Guard posses as painted in Frazier's book.

To write this book, Frazier has loaded his pen with colors of darkness and death—an odd palette when one considers the widespread popularity of this book: bloody blacks, unfriendly and untrustworthy browns, heartless reds, and gruesome and greedy greens and grays—to re-tell a tale told down through the Inman-Frazier family for over a hundred years as a later-day *Odyssey* offered up as a gauntlet of magic realism set in (un)real time and times that could be easily enough imagined but which seem almost paradoxically impossible to believe. Such a relentlessly gothic and at the same time dream-like (nightmarish) tale has rarely, if ever, been written since those by Poe on American soil. And never, I must say, (including Faulkner and Harper Lee) of such scale in the South.

As I look out the windows of my truck as we make our way up along the creeks and branches feeding the east fork of the Pidgeon River (Panther, Scapecat, Schoolhouse, Sorrell, Big) and up Inman Branch Road into the dark coves in the shadow of Cold Mountain, I don't see any of the huge native chestnuts that dominate the landscape of the book. Neither will I see or hear evidence before the day is done of the once-upon-a-time proliferation of red wolves and bears. These Haywood County woodlands (like most everywhere in the Southern Appalachian Blue Ridge) have been clear-cut and logged at least twice since Charles Frazier's Inman found his way back across the state of North Carolina to the western North Carolina mountains, having deserted the Confederate Army for more romantic adventure in the form of a long and natural life with the book's female protagonist Ada, who was waiting for him back home. Yet, even with the landscape greatly altered in these and other ways, one can still travel the narrow winding roads of the Cold Mountain watershed with a sense that he or she might still be traveling those roads in time, yet out of time, with the characters in Frazier's book. In many ways, little has changed, in that change has not made its way into this rugged and remote section of Haywood County where the Inman Chapel Union Church can still be seen almost as it was described in the early pages of the book, which direct descendants of book characters identified by their mid-late nineteenth century gravestones. Along this road, there are old log-framed barns and root cellars landscaped with solitary ancient apple trees down in a few bottoms that in Inman's days, would have been orchards and plowed fields. One can also see old dry-laid stone foundations now grown up in grass, where Inman and Ada might have sat on porch steps looking up at Cold Mountain by moonlight through a foggy mountain dusk.

As we follow Inman's journey home, and by the time he has crossed the state of North Carolina on foot, having fought several Homeric battles, as readers we feel like we have been through those battles too. And so, we are uplifted, if not relieved, as Inman makes his way into the mountains and down the ridge lines through Watauga County, Rutherford, Buncombe, and finally Haywood County and home.

> Inman walked through mountain country and kept to trails and saw few people. He measured out distance in portions of a day. A full day's walk. Half a day. Less than half a day. Anything shorter than that was just a little piece down the road. Miles and hours became concepts he disdained since he had not the means to measure either... As he studied on it, he recognized the line of every far ridge and valley to be more than remembered. They seemed long ago scribed indelible on his corneas with a sharp instrument. He looked out at this highland and knew the names of places and things.
>
> He said them aloud: Little Beartrail Ridge, Wagon Road Gap, Ripshin, Hunger Creek, Clawhammer Knob, Rocky Face. Not a mountain or watercourse lacked denomination.
>
> Not bird or bush anonymous. His place.

Nan and I are back on the road along the east fork of the Pidgeon, crossing Panther Branch and Ike Cove at the foot of Cold Mountain. We're on our way out 215 to the north where we hit 276 west into Waynesville and then around the long way home.

It's the fall of 1997. The history of the past and the present have been united in the creek bottoms and the balds beneath the summit of Cold Mountain on this day, as we cross Balsam Gap into Jackson county on the four-lane to Sylva. In the past, we have left Inman dead in Ada's arms in a cove on the back side of Cold Mountain looking down from the Shining Rock Wilderness. In the present, we are headed to the flood plains of the Tuckaseigee River in the Little Canada community where we will bide our time with the memory of Frazier's unlikely classic, waiting through a winter in real time for word of his next book.

No Dharma

Thomas Berry's *The Great Work*

Maybe once every one hundred years does someone emerge from the shuddering mass of humanity who speaks to us with a kind of clarity that is universally profound. Thomas Berry is such a figure. Sometimes referred to as an *ecologian*, and having authored important books on world religions as well as the seminal Sierra Club book, *The Dream of the Earth*, he has devoted his life to the study of spirituality and the natural world with a focus on stewardship of community, conscience, and the commons (wilderness). Berry, a North Carolina native now at age ninety three, has written a book that, for it's times, could easily be considered the modern equivalent of the biblical book of *Revelations*. But unlike the hallucinogenic prophesy of *Revelations*, *The Great Work* is a vision of sober apostasy and common sense. And while the implications, here, are universal, the approach and the language is very much of human scale. Berry's perceptions and premonitions are grounded heavily in scholarship and fact. There is no translation or catechism needed to grasp the essence of this book only an open mind and a strong heart.

While it is hard to know exactly where to begin to write about this book, so very rich in keen, clear associations, prophetic observation, apocryphal warning and salient solutions, we can begin with the major thesis of the book: to identify the role of the human community in relation to the other components of the planet, and the discontinuity between human and nonhuman life forms and modes of being—where all the rights and all inherent values are given to the human. Here, Berry simply states that it is because of the lack of limits placed on the human community with regard to "progress" and "development" (what he identifies as "no dharma") that there is now a tremendous threat to

57

the well-being of other life forms and systems, which are the basis for our own existence.

Despite the fact that Berry says that the current Earth/human predicament is the gravest in the entire history of the planet's existence (imperative enough to have coined a name for the cusp of a new historical/biological era—the *Ecozoic*) this is not a book of doom and gloom. Rather, this is a book that tells it like it is and then delineates a course of action to begin to set things right. And while the book's title might seem to be something of an indulgent superlative, you can believe me when I say that this is anything but the case. Even though Berry is direct and firm in his observations and insinuations as to the current Earth predicament and the failings of the human species in the past two to three hundred years, he approaches his subject with a nascent humility and reverence which never undermine or belie the credibility of his argument as fact. Berry gives us, in *The Great Work*, a front row seat for viewing the Earth that is, as he says, "a single reality composed of diversity beyond all understanding and description. And it is in this diversity that we find both the Earth's endless wonder and its functional integrity."

The Great Work is, on one hand, a cogent thesis on the power possessed by industrial civilizations and their ability to disrupt the integral functioning of the life systems of the Earth, and on the other hand, a brilliant bit of sunshine shed on those problems in terms of suggestions for solutions toward returning the Earth to its state of natural beauty and the human populations to a necessary sense of wonder. This is a vision for the future that includes a functioning Earth as perceived as being a symphony, a tapestry, a painting—a "creative equilibrium." Here, Berry suggests a simple, single word solution to our current problems which stem from relating to the Earth as subject rather than object: *intimacy*. Intimacy in the sense of a renewed and reinvigorated relationship with our natural surrounding and a new attitude of respect for all non-human life forms which includes the Earth itself. It is only this sort of intimacy, he says, that can save us, quite literally, from ourselves.

In a sometimes disturbing book where almost every line is quotable and every other line profound, Berry has penned a more hopeful tome than his predecessor, Patmos's St. John. As something of a modern day Aquinas, he leads us through the history of global biocide and geocide perpetrated by nation states and transnational corporations, then he outlines in detail the necessary steps toward recovery based on a sense of ethics and responsibility. "Currently," he says, "we are applying micro-phase solutions to macro-phase problems." And he continues— "Concern for the environment must become the central organizing principal of civilization!"

"It will take a conversion of the human psyche," Berry says about our current dilemma and what it will take to get things back on track and moving toward finding ourselves in a state of balance with the natural world and the universe. "In our creating a kind of *Wonderworld* with our industries and technologies, we have, in fact, created a *Wasteworld* in which there has evolved a strange paradox by which our efforts to establish a thoroughly sanitized world have led to our current toxic world." He qualifies this by emphatically pointing out that our resistance to any kind of imposed "limitation" placed on our march of progress and development has perpetrated this downward spiral of equilibrium on the planet. What we have done lately, he chides, is to try to compensate for over two hundred years of destruction by establishing a study and plan for "sustainable development," a concept that is a contradiction in terms, as development is simply not sustainable at this point in human/Earth history. "We must have a paradigm shift in culture to contend with the present dilemma," says Berry. "We must reinvent the human itself!"

In the end, Berry says that our myopic and anthropocentric relationship with the Earth has led us to a situation that is unparalleled in the multi-million-year history of the Earth, and it is only in our willingness to embrace and reorient ourselves to the natural heritage of our existence, to the biorhythms of the natural world, to a perspective that incorporates community and bioregions back into our cultural lifestyles, that there is any hope for our future survival. Bleak news, this, but not impossible to surmount, he says, if we are willing to take the conscious and meticulous steps needed toward reorienting our social systems (government, religions, universities and commercial-industrial corporations) toward the teaching and practice of this more "ecological and universal paradigm."

What can one say, except: If there is a single book that you buy this year, make it *The Great Work*. We owe it to ourselves and if we are to believe Thomas Berry, we owe it to the Earth that has sustained human life for, lo, these thousands of years. If one by one we can inform ourselves, then one by one we can make a difference. *The Great Work*, I believe, will be remembered in the future as the touchstone, the "bible" whose wisdom laid the groundwork for our continued healthy existence here on Earth. This may be overly optimistic and is high praise, I know, but not delirious, as on this subject there has never been a better or more important book.

The Last Luddite
Technology and the Price of the Future

For years my friends have been saying to me: "You're living in the Ice Age" with regard to my refusal to accept and embrace computers and the new on-line technologies that have invaded our landscape at the pace of a run away glacier retreating, unchecked, from its Pleistocene prison of frozen snow. My seemingly un-retractable stance has had as much to do with principal and ideology as it has with the fact that I am physically incompatible with this world, the feel and the look, of these new machines. But, it wasn't merely a snobbishness born of ineptness in dealing with machinery that was the genesis of my stubbornness. I truly have believed that this new unquestioned fascination with information and speed is a threat to my genetic coding—the agrarian and environmental sympathies and sensibilities that are ingrained in me as part of who I am. This attitude, more than anything, played a major role in my taking the unpopular stand of refusing to become a rider on the Information Superhighway. To be and to remain cyber-free. The last Luddite.

As a writer, in many ways, by remaining true to my love of organic simplicity where the writing process is concerned, I have been gradually putting myself out of work, as the rest of the writing field has embraced the computerization of the word almost to the complete exclusion of anything else. "What's the rush?" has always been my reactionary battle cry when confronted by hyper-active editors who demand submission of plastic disks or text transferred to them via e-mail. Until recently, I've been able to accomplish my own personal needs as a self-supporting freelance writer without having to give in to the God of Speed. In the literary world, I am the tortoise, not the hare.

But, for the sake of clarity, let's go back to the beginning— I was raised in the woods. Surrounded by National Forests, Wilderness Refuges, Wild and Scenic Rivers. There was a seemingly infinite amount of natural space that surrounded me no matter in which direction I might have wandered forth from my boyhood home in Graham County. The woods, the wilderness was my playground and my source of entertainment. The deep woods was where I built my made-of-dead-limbs and moss-covered "forts" and "clubhouses," as well as a place where there was an endless horizon of potential for exploration and discovery. The branches, streams and creeks were my swimming pools and sources for many a miniature beaver-like dam. The fields, slicks and balds were the gridirons, ball-fields, and tracks—where my friends and I congregated for group games and sports. A veritable gymnasium of the out-of-doors. With this as the stage for my upbringing and the profound experience of my formative years, is it any wonder, then, that I would be discontented, in replacement, with anything else?

Subsequent years, following my departure from the Mountain South, spent in large towns and then in cities of ever-increasing size and population, while being stimulating in terms of things encountered for the first time, were, in the end, a disappointment, with claustrophobia setting in quickly and permanently after the novelty had worn off. Nothing else, it seemed, could fill my need to be surrounded by space. Lots of space. Space full of things that were wild, and free.

One of my favorite quotes from Henry David Thoreau is, "All good things are wild and free." As our wild spaces are ever-increasingly becoming the domain of urban and suburban sprawl, we find ourselves faced with certain choices, certain decisions. Decisions that carry with them the questioning adage of "to do, or not to do," as we choose sides between the inalienable rights of the environment versus those of human progress.

In much of Europe there are already strict recycling laws in place. Germany, for instance, has made recycling mandatory for everyone. Computers, with their short life spans and with the endless amount of attachments and software that make up the "nuclear family" of the technology, have become one of the biggest problems of suburban sprawl, as everyone's used computers end up in the land-fill. With the tremendous boom in the computer business, there are literally, in this country alone, mountains of computers and their "offspring" filling the limited space that's been set aside for trash. But Germany has seen the light and has written and enforced a law against the throwing away of computers. It is mandatory, therefore, that computers are recycled back into the industry and emerge, reincarnated, as newer models, racks of reinvented software, isles of nouveaux modems and printers.

Let's go back, here, to my earlier insinuations concerning the impact of new computer technology on human health. My "environmental impact statement" on this subject includes recently-documented finding from studies (including a couple of single-sample, blind study experiments of my own) that say that the cumulative time spent in front of a computer terminal has significant negative impact on the general eyesight of users, that there is potential crippling muscular and neuro-muscular residual effects from keyboard use, that attention span and reading (book reading) capacities are diminished and/or dramatically compromised from chronic computer usage, and that there is a direct correlation to attention deficit and increased memory loss (especially in the area of what I would call "common sense memory" or genetic memory in relation to survival in the natural world). All this, not to mention the fact that I personally question the safeness of sitting a foot or more from a screen, for long periods of time, that is emitting potentially harmful low-level radiation!

From where I sit, here in the Little Canada–Tuckaseigee watershed of Jackson County, there would seem to be some very real questions that haven't been answered as to whether or not this new computer technology is, in fact, more a threat than an asset as we, collectively, distance ourselves farther and farther from nature and our natural inheritance as consciously evolving mammals.

Like every tragedy worth its salt, there is a denouement and a fall from grace. My personal fall from grace was born of the mother of invention: necessity. And it was a fall from a great height that was accompanied by much pain—reminiscent of the experience I had in coming out of the woods in late 1982 after living a wild and self-sufficient back-to-the-land lifestyle for almost four years—where I was met with a tremendous wall of popular culture. A similar cautionary tale, also without the literary device of a *deus ex machina*, was played out in reverse when I sat down in front of a computer after a painful period of instruction, to become one of the converted. This, too, was a huge shock to my system. And even though I knew that I needed this technology to do what needed to be done (namely to organize and produce an enormous public-relations event in behalf of the fight in the western North Carolina mountains for clean air), I fought it tooth and nail.

As I logged hour upon hour on the keyboard of my Hewlett Packard, gazing into the monitor like it was a crystal ball, I was, on the inside, beating myself up. "You hypocrite!" "Wimp!" "Sheep!" "Turncoat!" "Jesabelle!" I wondered, and still do, just how far over the "buffalo jump" edge of no return I've gone, and whether I have, like so many millions of others, been duped into thinking that all this technology is inevitable and that it's necessary to our future, while all the while alterations are occurring in the mind that render us even incapable of making the kind of clear and objective associations and conclusions necessary to a healthy sense of critical awareness.

Just in time to save me from committing some sort of cyberspace hari-kari, my Indiana friend Johnathan Watson sends me an e-mail, reading my mind and saying, "You don't compromise your Thoreauvian stance by using these machines. You can have your cake and click it too." Clever, I thought, but is it true?

Well, the beat goes on, as the song says, and after sending one hundred and fifty e-mails, transposing a novel, a translation manuscript and a collection of poems face to face with the monster that is "the machine," I'm truly, now, a *bona fide* member of the Information Generation, albeit a middle-aged one and often raging. That "Ice Age" I was accused of living in has, in quick order, melted into some sort of virtual past, and I am hardly the hold out, renegade or outlaw I once was. But, like the Lone Ranger must have felt, I, too, have experienced the lone-liness and the pathos of being the "last" Luddite. And I want you to know that there are still days when I am only a squeeze of my hair-trigger away from sending my monitor to Boot Hill and returning to my friends in the Hole in the Wall gang, where I'll again be cyber free. Where life goes on amidst natural surroundings, moving slow—the way the old timers say it ought to be.

The New Naturalists

(The Southern Appalachian Mountains
Are The Place To Look)

Such an ocean of wooded, waving, swelling mountain beauty and grandeur is not to be described. Countless forest-clad hills, side by side in rows and groups—all united by curves and slopes of inimitable softness and beauty. Oh, these forest gardens of our Father! What perfection, what divinity, in their architecture!
> — John Muir (*Travels*) of his first impressions of the mountains of western North Carolina

With issues such as development, zoning and land-use legislation, toxic waste and air pollution almost constantly in the news these days here in western North Carolina, I've been thinking about this business of the desecration of the environment, and who it might be that is going to lead us out of this self-destructive paradigm that was set into motion with the Industrial Revolution and has continued to gather momentum in the last century and a half with the rise of free-market capitalism. Where are the "dirt-doctors," the "earth-healers"? I keep asking myself. Where are the great charismatic voices in government that might begin the work of turning things around? And if not in government, then in the culture in general—where are our leaders? It seems that when looking in all the obvious places, there is no one addressing the really pressing questions of our day: overpopulation, development, preservation, free-trade capitalism.

It seems to me that it has always been the naturalists who have led the way toward a more progressive thinking where questions of balance and sustainability are concerned, that it is the nature writers who have positioned themselves on the front lines of the myriad battles to save and preserve the environment. It is the nature writers who have sown the seeds that would sprout as ecological movements, private foundations and governmental programs focused on the long view where the welfare of the country's and the planet's landscape is concerned. Past generations have looked to the work of Emerson, Thoreau, Burroughs, Muir, Bartram, Kephart, Leopold, Carson, Eisley... and then, even more recently, to writers like Robinson Jeffers, Gary Snyder, and, finally, to the South in writers like Wendell Berry of the Kentucky backcountry and farm communities (who has written exquisitely on local culture and community for the better part of a lifetime in such books as *The Unsettling of America* and *The Gift of Good Land*), and Thomas Berry (a North Carolina native, who, in his books *The Dream of the Earth* and *The Great Work*, has captured the imagination of the whole environmental movement with his elevated message of spiritual ecology). Following in their footsteps, is a new generation and a new breed of gifted Southern nature writers.

"If you would learn the secrets of nature," Thoreau wrote, "you must practice more humanity than others." That credo, more or less, sums up the ethos of these "new naturalists." They are not only talking the talk, they are walking the walk. They are not only writing an engaged prose and poetry that evokes the spirit of "The Old Naturalists" and their tenants for a sustainable future, but are quite literally engaged in a kind of activism that is, at once, journalistic and/or literary and biographical. They are, through their work and deeds, inspiring, organizing and participating in non-violent "actions" and activities that provide alternatives to community apathy and destruction of natural habitat.

While most of the writers of name have and continue to come from the northeast, mid-west, or west coast, the South has "risen up" to give the other sections of the country a run for its money. Here in the mountains of the Southern Appalachians—in and around the area of the Great Smoky Mountains National Park—live an exceptional group of dedicated, if not devout, '60s-generation nature writers worthy of national attention. In a region where the issues of air pollution, water quality, extinction of floral and faunal species, and loss of traditional cultures are front and center, this handful of remarkable writers are not only making a mark on the genre of environmental non-fiction, but are making a difference.

This group of "Southern Nature" writers is anchored in Athens, Georgia by the Southern Nature Writers Gatherings and the University of Georgia Press. Seniored by such voices as those of Jim Kilgo and Franklin Burroughs, are a younger cadre of eco-activist writers and poets who have joined ranks with their elder kinsmen to form a Southern Nature Writers contingent that has served notice and is setting the Southeast, if not the rest of the nation on fire. Writers such as Chrisopher Camuto, Bill Belleville, Janisse Ray, John Lane, Roger Pinckney, Susan Cerulean, Jan DeBlieu, Dorinda Dahlmeyer, Ann Fisher-Wirth and Julie Hauserman being essential to this southern brigade.

Recently, a few of this elite group have gotten well-deserved recognition from their leadership as well as their work and are singled out, here, like flags unfurled, to hold up to the rest of the country and its various writers and regions. If there is anyone who has embraced and embodied the writing of Thoreau and Kephart it is the recluse of the group, George Ellison. As someone who has lived for some time without electricity and running water over in his Swain County, North Carolina home—in a cabin only approachable by foot—his knowledge of nature lore and Native American history in this region is approaching the level of being encyclopedic. His newspaper columns, his frequent nature-walk workshops, his books, and his contributions to the living folklore of the region have been and continue to be invaluable in educating the public about its past as well as it's invasive present. His stamp appears on two of the seminal tomes of Southern Appalachian cultural history: Mooney's *The Myths of the Cherokee*, and Kephart's

Our Southern Highlanders, for which he has been bestowed with the honor of being asked to write new, updated introductions.

Just next door, in Jackson County, whitewater enthusiast, wilderness and recreation writer and poet John Lane spends his summers in a remote cove off John's Creek Road in the Caney Fork section of Cullowhee in a beautiful traditionally-reconstructed one-room saw-mill shack built by fifth-generation Macon County native Keith Monteith, and is actively involved in water and land development issues in the region, while writing a book on the Chattooga River. His journal-entry book *Weed Time,* which was written in the environs of Whittier while living up Camp Creek Road at the old Jim Smith nursery, is a snapshot, or better yet, a petroglyph of place-based awareness. His investigative journalism work in behalf of ecological issues here in the mountains and down on the other side of the "Blue Wall" in the South Carolina piedmont in Spartanburg County are written, thoughtfully, in attack mode, leaving no stone unturned. While his journalistic work is clever, aggressive and geologic, his poetry written here in and about these mountains is equally, in the other direction, gentle, sensitive, fluid.

Waking in the Blue Ridge

In the animal light of early morning
dreams persist but I am quickly
victim to the world's precision —
how oaks become one
in a web of blue above,
and the fox bursts
toward the nested quail,
or in tricks of color
copperheads coil
where they could not be.

All this in the hour
before breakfast, in the heaven
of unnoticed verdancy and light.

And then there is Christopher Camuto, whose writing on fly-fishing, red wolves and the Great Smoky Mountain National Park is the stuff of supernovas. His rise to prominence as a Southern Appalachian nature writer has been meteoric. His whip-cracking intellect and inspired vocabulary have been a wake-up call for other writers and for readers of regional and natural history. His combined mix of an auto-biographical and objective writing style is the next best thing to "being there." The visual images he creates with language go way beyond being merely "photographic." They linger and last in the mind's eye—for months and years on end. His book *Another Country: Journeying Toward the Cherokee Mountains* (re-released by the University of Georgia Press) is, in my opinion, one of the best books ever written about western North Carolina.

> I think of the virtues of the animals that became the founding spirits
> for the Cherokee clans. I think of the autumn dance of white-tails in
> the rut and the delicate way bears walk. I think of the stillness of
> trout, of the silver of moving water. I thing of the masks that animals
> wear that became the masks of those dancers, of the way men learned
> to drum on hollow logs like grouse, to pipe like wood thrush, to
> weave like spiders, to fashion baskets light as spruce cones, to
> scream in battle like ravens, to hunt like wolves.

Janisse Ray, a native Georgia "cracker," who is struggling to save the southern Long Leaf Pine, as well as her family farm, from extinction, is the author of the award-winning book *The Ecology of a Cracker Childhood.* Janisse is the youngest of our regional cadre of new naturalist writer/activists, but may be the rising star of the group. Her charisma, her immutable will, her strong sense of the feminine, her gameliness and grit coupled with a very disciplined and poetic relationship with language, makes her the kind of show-stopper the environmental movement needs in order to bring attention to important issues.

Not only has she turned many heads in a nature-writing literary world dominated by men, with her striking good looks, but has turned heads with her dexterity and integrity in such poems as the following from her collection titled *Naming the Unseen* which pays tribute to the place of her origins:

Bone Deposit

When I am dead, put my bones in Georgia
that made them. Give back the calcium,
phosphorous, the holy manganese that serve
me well — keepers of this unruly flesh.
When I am dead, let me honor land that
struck fire within and offered to hot and
hungry air a skeleton pieced of earth
that holds me aloft in the spinning and
spiraling of this world. The elements of
bones compel me. I return time and
again to feel her soil, wondering what I
search for, what hauls me back: ossein of
day-myths, compound of marrow percolating
subterranean veins, debt that will be freed.

In addition to these high-profile, rising stars of the "Southern Nature" cadre, there is an ever-expanding core group of cultural and environmental activists here in the mountains working alongside one another to create some sort of bioregional awareness as well as a sense of responsibility for our regional ecosystem. During the 1980s and early 1990s, the beast-of-burden of this movement was a publication called *Katuah Journal* and its loyal, hard-working heart of *pro-bono* editors and writers. Espousing the values, ethics and hands-on particulars of the Bioregional and Green movements, *Katuah*'s main emphasis was on teaching and its main vehicle was the newspaper—which, until its demise in the early 1990s, had a focused mixture of articles on plant lore, environmental issues, gardening and farming tips, regional geographic history, Native American culture.

More recently, however, the movement for a sustained environment has been enjoined by anthropologist/writer/activist Harvard Ayers at Appalachian State University—whose work in books such as *An Appalachian Tragedy: Air Pollution and Tree Death in The Eastern Forests of North America* (Sierra Club) and *Polluted Parks in Peril: The Five Most Air-Polluted Parks in the United States* as well as his work in behalf of clean air coalitions here in western North Carolina has been influential, if not essential to the recent passage of the groundbreaking "Clean Smokestacks Act," setting a precedent for the rest of the country.

What do all these writers have in common? They have all, at some time, if not often, appeared in the pages of a visionary news weekly that is the brainchild of founder and publisher/editor Scott McLeod, called *The Smoky Mountain News*. The team of staff writer Don Hendershot and publisher Scott McLeod have made *The Smoky Mountain News* a much-needed addition and mainstay to the more conservatively traditional and "old school" papers that fall short in claiming to be the environmental voice of the people in the western mountains. *The Smoky Mountain News*, with its diligence and thoughtful writing, week in and week out, on the subject of the environment, has served to not only educate but to focus attention on the many issues here in the region whereas the health and balance of things natural are concerned.

While the amount of work to be done in cleaning up our environment here in the southern Blue Ridge Mountains might, at times, seem overwhelming, these "new naturalists" and others like them are, I'm convinced, equal to the task. This is a focused and dedicated bunch who have taken on the heavy yoke of unchecked "progress," "growth" and "development," and with strong shoulders are pulling the ecology wagon in which the rest of the nation rides. "May it continue...." as the old Cherokee ceremonial chant goes: this nature-activist tradition, this beautiful place, and these people who live here well.

May it Continue

for Joy Harjo

May the brown earth and the green leaves
thrive in color and in grace.
May it continue.

May the clear air and the cumulocirrus clouds
be there in the sky and in each breath, always.
May it continue.

May the water made of sweet minerals and salt
in small streams and large rivers
flow forever and forever flow to the seas.
May it continue.

May the sun shine warm and bright
and the moon give light at night—*shinning from shook foil.*
May it continue.

May the beautiful birds of Hawaii and
the luminous parrots of Peru fly far and fast
and may their number grow.
May it continue.

May the deer and the elk, the antelope and the ibis
move and migrate, leap and lope across plain
and wooded plateau.
May it continue.

May the whale and the dolphin and the manatee
swim deep in dark oceans and lagoons and sing.
May it continue.

May the elephants forever in families roam,
trunk to tail, trumpeting bliss.
May it continue.

May waves of warm frost linger in bush and blaze
that puts fire in the peat of loam. And let lick cry from ripe vine.
May it continue.

May the rose climb through
the cold murmur of morning dirt.
May dark mulch coax tendrils from sleep.
May it continue.

May wild words come flying on green coils and
may juice in rock rustle with blue moss
in the sound of song.
May it continue.

II

THE END OF EDEN

Articles & Editorials

① Trunks o+65?
② rhododendrons-ch+dbn.
③ mud - 6 sq wat
④ water (m+d)
⑤ underwater sth

Beaver Dam on old Johns River Rd.

Beaver activity has moved on down the creek.

hairs on veins under leaves

Polygonatum (1' high)
pubescens
(Hairy Solomon seal)

silt has been trapped on the logs of the dam and it has become quite solid. Four years ago I couldn't walk across it. Now it is very solid.

— birch is the main tree
The beavers seem to prefer
— small fish jumping in pond.

Ground Ivy — Creeping Charlie
glephoma hederacea

Julian Price Park   Robert Johnson 5/26/06

77

A Road to Nowhere

The War on the Environment
in Western North Carolina

In recent years, western North Carolina and the areas in and around the Great Smokies National Park have become an environmental battleground. I returned to the mountains in 1978, expecting to find the kind of relatively clean air, clean water and undeveloped landscape of my youth. Instead, I found myself in the midst of the beginnings of an all-out war on the ecology of the region, which, today, has escalated and manifested itself in any number of ways and around any number of issues. This battleground does serve, however, as an instructive micro-cosmic model for the rest of the country, with issues ranging every-where from an EPA Superfund Site in Haywood County to the "Road to Nowhere" controversy in Graham and Swain counties, farther west.

Like modern-day Paul Reveres, a growing number of watchdog en-vironmental organizations in the region have seen ecologically-based issues arise, like invading armies—by land, air and sea—and have hung out their warning lanterns in the belfries of public concern.

By land—The 1980s and 1990s saw battle-lines drawn between environmentalists and the Forest Service and then the logging and timber companies in the region, over the issues of clear-cut logging (especially on Forest Service land), chip mills and the permanent preservation of wilderness (best evidenced in the "Blue Wall," Duke Power sale). More recently, the DOT, Boards of County Commission-ers and business have drawn their respective lines in the dirt with environmental groups and the Eastern Band of the Qualla Boundary Cherokee over the issues of a major land swap between the Eastern Band and the National Park Service, as well as the controversial "Road to Nowhere"—a four-lane road that is cutting a giant swath through the

Smokies as well as threatening a portion of the Fontana watershed in Swain County.

By air—The air quality issue has raised its ugly head here in the mountains in recent years, with the NOx readings threatening to reach levels as high as any in the entire country, including such record-setting metropolitan areas as Los Angeles—necessitating the creation of a variety of Quality Control organizations as well as such grassroots activist environmental organizations as the newly-formed Canary Coalition, which is working to coordinate existing environmental groups and to organize media events such as a planned "Air Aid" concert/event featuring high-profile stars from the worlds of music, entertainment, business and politics.

By sea—There is the on-going Pigeon River controversy. A hard-fought battle between Champion Paper Company and a coalition of river awareness and preservation groups in the western part of the state as well as eastern Tennessee. Added to this, are several community and county-based quality control groups monitoring river and streams, development impact, and city water systems.

While land, culture, history and community have always been important cornerstones of life here in the Smoky Mountains, never has the debate been hotter or the threat greater to the very existence of these preternatural themes of rural mountain life. While there has always been a certain amount of conflict involved in the history of the Mountain South, never before has the landscape been so littered with controversy of an environmental nature. At every turn we see communities at odds with one another over the over-riding question of the bottom line vs. preservation of the environment. (Witness the recent withdrawal of Haywood County from the Haywood/Buncombe Air Quality Compact.) In this respect, the Great Smokies can be seen as something of a microcosm for the rest of the country with regard to not only the escalation of existing environmental issues, but the multiplicity of issues, now, collectively, coming to a head in the region.

While the residents of Big Cove over on the Qualla Reservation are feuding with the Swain County Board of Commissioners (reminiscent of the Indian/European conflicts from the 19th century, and before) over the land-swap deal with the Forest Service, the "Road to Nowhere" is rapidly becoming a paradoxical metaphor for local comic relief. Meanwhile, EVERYONE is breathing some of the foulest air in the nation—a scenario already having documented health-related repercussions on all ages of the population. "We're like the canaries in the coal mines," says Canary Coalition Director Avram Freidman of Sylva. "Without being asked, we're all being used as canaries while our air in being eroded by the power and coal companies and the auto industry."

While the various battle lines are being drawn and sides taken, the landscape, culture, history and sense of community here in the western North Carolina mountains is changing—changing rapidly, and one would sense, inextricably, forever. One can only hope that these kinds of changes are not fatal to the unique and long-standing cultures, along with plant and animal populations indigenous to the Smokies, and that such recent action as the All-Taxa Survey[2] being carried out in the Great Smoky Mountains National Park will provide the necessary information, leading to a baseline model and antidotes for the waning ecosystem health of what is a true treasure-trove of biodiversity. Let us hope that this widening road of conflict will not, in the end, be known only as a road that led "nowhere," but will become, instead, a road that will be perceived to have led to "somewhere." Somewhere beautiful. Again.

---

[2] an effort to enumerate *all* life forms within the Park — the Smokies All Taxa Biodiversity Inventory (ATBI).

It Can Happen to You

I. It Can Happen To You

January has not only been a cold month in Tuckasegee, it's also been the herald of some cold news. Just as I was beginning to feel snug, safe, and secure out here in the Little Canada community, of late, reading about the 4400 acre housing development being planned for Balsam Mountain on the other side of the county, first word comes of a similar 2000-plus-acre land deal that has taken place over on the Bear Lake reservoir only a few miles further down Highway 281 from where I live. "Getting a little too close for comfort," I think as I hear the news of the Bear Lake development for the first time. Still, our river bottom farming valley in the flood plain where the Tuckaseigee River meets the overflow stream from Lake Glenville seems far enough away from Bear Lake and therefore protected from the specter of subdivisions or any real threat to the tranquil life to which we have become accustomed. With the exception of an occasional gunshot, the occasional power saw and the early morning and late afternoon traffic along 281, almost all I hear or see on any given day here in my haven are the sounds and sights of the natural world.

I moved to the Tuckasegee community because of the ambiance of the rural farming lifestyle, and the close access to wilderness, and because it was one of the last sections of Jackson County with affordable housing—affordable, that is, for someone like myself who lives on what he can grow and scrape together as a writer trying to make ends meet in the midst of America's consumer culture. The natural world and quiet neighbors feed my solitary needs as a writer, as does my large garden feed my body as well as supplying me with a small income from the supplemental food which I can sell. These things, this place, keep

82

soul and body alive. When I moved here in 1993, I truly felt that this place would sustain me in these kinds of ways for the rest of my life. The urban sprawl moving this way from Sylva, fifteen miles away, would never reach the Canada community in my lifetime, I prophesized at the time.

Around the time of the turning of the new year, while up in the study I have set up for myself in the attic of this old farmhouse, doing some writing, I was distracted by the noise of voices and the sounds of hammers on steel. A quick glance out the window revealed surveyors driving painted metal corner posts in the ground at the end of my driveway, tying up bright blue and orange plastic ribbon to the trees on the far side of the drainage ditch that defines the western edge of the property. I interrupted my work and went outside to see what the hell was going on. A friendly conversation with the survey foreman told me more than I wanted to know—the eighty-eight acres of pasture, woods and mountain next to me had been bought by a land development outfit based in Tarpon Springs, Florida that was planning on converting the river bottom land and adjoining woods into a housing sub-development of fifteen or more lots. In a few minutes time, my happy little life in "Eden" had become more like something from the pages of "Paradise Lost." So much for "the poet as prophet."

Instead of the sweet sound of the hundreds of birds that sit in the old ash and pine trees that surround my old farmhouse singing, the yelps of foxes up in the holler, and the rushing sounds of the Tuckasei-gee as it flows beside the road that runs in front of the house, I must now accept for the indefinite future, in replacement, the sound of chainsaws, skill saws and human noise—unnatural and unfriendly sounds that will serve to disturb my solitude as well as my sleep.

II. The Facts

Since that fateful January day, I've spent a lot of time reading the editorial section of all the local newspapers, talking to activists and advocates of land-use regulations—trying to get a realistic picture of exactly what has been happening to Jackson County during my long idealistic sleep. What I have uncovered is disturbing. In terms of my "prophesy" of living out my remaining years here in Tuckasegee untouched by the outside world, the future looks bleak.

As Scott McLeod has written in one of his recent editorials in the *Smoky Mountain News* and as Mark Jamison writes with controlled emotion in a concurrent letter to the editor in the *Sylva Herald*, Jackson County is experiencing a period of unprecedented growth, in the process of which we are losing our culture and our way of life. Small farms and family holdings are disappearing. In their place are appearing housing developments that neither the old people or young families will be able to afford. My trips to the Offices of Mapping, Records and Deeds at the Jackson County Justice Center tell the story of the development boom here in Jackson County. In a printout of aggregate land sales of 40 acres or more over the past year, I have been able to identify clearly no less than a dozen land development companies that have bought land in various parts of Jackson County. None of these companies have bought parcels of land that is anything less than 117 acres, with the high end of the list being the projected development areas down the road at Bear Lake (2400 acres) and the much written about Balsam Mountain Preserve (4400 acres). Much to my consternation, six of these purchases by land development corporations have taken place here in the Canada community, as well as six more purchases by named individuals for large parcels—all of which may be targeted for new housing development for all I know.

In the past year, alone, there are on record 46 land purchases here in Jackson County of forty acres or more with a spread from $2000 an acre in the remoter sections of the county, up to as much as $200,000 or more an acre in the Cashiers community, and with whopping price tags of $9,600,000 and $9,300,000 having been paid for the Balsam Mountain Preserve and the Bear Lake developments respectively.[3] Staring

---

[3] These prices have gone up exponentially since this article was first published in 2002.

down the barrel of this multi-barreled gun, what do those of us who live in Jackson County have to look forward to? What kind of picture does this paint?

For those who have been here for generations or have, like myself, moved here because of a slower, simpler lifestyle, we are now facing a perplexing, if not troubling, future. A future where what we have known in terms of heritage, community and the environment may, and most likely will be (unless certain preventative actions are taken) changed radically, forever. Here, where science and psychology have not yet replaced geography, place names and genealogies that have been a means of orientation and identity for those who have lived in these hills, will disappear, will be replaced by something proscribed and homogenous, foreign and from the outside. These natives, as well as myself and others who have come here in more recent years as "new natives" and have put down roots in order to pry our attention away from the squalor, fear and brutality of the urban life, can look forward to waking up one morning in the not-too-distant future to a world of base commerce, overpopulation and a drone-like, money-driven culture that has moved in here from Florida, Texas and New York.

What happens when the community that has, for generations, been Little Canada becomes, suddenly, "Little Cashiers"? When Gill's Grill at the intersection of 107 and 281 becomes a Sushi Bar, and Ken's Shell Station becomes a cappuccino café? Before we allow things to progress this far we must take a deeper look at the overall situation and the options that are available to us. "At this stage in the population and building boom in western North Carolina, we need to begin using the "z" word (zoning) as a consideration and possible alternative to un-checked development," says Sylva business owner and Tuckasegee Branch of the Western North Carolina Alliance Chairman, Avram Friedman. "Historically, there has been a large populist lobby against zoning in western North Carolina, and for the most part for good reasons."

But things are much different now than they were even ten years ago, and the threat from outside development interests is a much greater one that can, now, no longer be ignored. Obscure, romantic bygone notions of individual independence must give way to a larger, enlightened vision of the greater good whereas land management is concerned. No one of us is more important than the community as a whole, and the whole community of Jackson County is now being threatened from the outside by not only air pollution, but by unchecked land development, as well."

"We all have a right to live here, no matter what our economic status," echoes Mark Jamison, newly appointed member of the Jackson County Commissioners Planning Board and a vocal advocate of land management regulations. "With these kinds of developments increasing property values, some say that this rising tide lifts all boats. I would counter that this rising tide swamps more boats than it lifts. In making our decisions about managing growth, preserving the environment, or protecting the county, these decisions should be judged against one standard—do they protect people or profit."

III. Smart Growth

While the problem of stopping, even managing, growth is an ominous one (especially if we consider the escalating world-wide problem of overpopulation), we here in Jackson County may be part of the last line of defense in protecting our region from a fate that has befallen the coastal corridors and large interior cities of the rest of the country. To achieve this, political, business and activist groups need to pinpoint environmental quality as a key to the county's overall quality of life and begin designing strategies linking the conservation of open lands and ecosystems to productive landscapes, agriculture, recreation, and tourism. By mixing private and public approaches to conservation and development, Jackson County and western North Carolina as a whole can look beyond narrow legal or regulatory re-sponses to their environmental and social challenges and instead im-pliment an assortment of flexible, responsive techniques. One of the main focuses of this process would be maintaining an affordable cost of living for full-time residents.

Here in Jackson County, a first step toward resolution of these problems has been taken with the on-going "Smart Growth" public hearings and workshop sessions that have given a public forum and a voice to concerned residents of our county regarding the subdivision development issue and other concerns regarding community, environment and culture. In the fifth Smart Growth session held at the Sylva Justice Center, the assembled crowd voted the issues of "preservation of the county's natural beauty" and "preservation of rural character" as their top priorities and concerns. The second largest number of votes went to the issues of the preservation of the county's water and air. In terms of strategies cited to deal with these concerns, Land Use Planning received a high percentage of votes—an indication, at least to this writer, that positive progress is already being made.

While critical issues are beginning to be addressed, as always the bottom line is with legislation. Our local and state representatives in government need to know where we stand on this issue of development and need to be held accountable. While western North Carolina will never become a carbon copy of domino development horrors in places like Newark, New Jersey, its individual horrors could well be visited upon us. Before that happens we need to lend our voices to the outcry against unchecked land development. We need to act.

In his classic book on environmental ethics *The Great Work*, ecologian Thomas Berry states simply: "We hear a lot of talk these days from political committee members and real estate lobbyists about 'sustainable development' as a solution to the growth issue. This is a feel-good spin that attempts to instill in us a false sense of ease concerning some very troubling issues. The term 'sustainable development' is an oxymoron, a contradiction in terms. In our present predicament, any expanded 'development' will not be able to be sustained. There are already too many people per square mile on this planet than the planet can carry, can hold. How can we increase development, continue to populate, and be able to sustain ourselves with even the very basics of human necessity?"

IV. Epilogue

Meanwhile, back on Highway 281 here in Tuckasegee, while I have been writing this piece, I have seen more surveyors, heavy equipment contractors, builders, and potential buyers scouting the 88.3 acres adjoining the land where I live. It's only a matter of time before the bulldozers and the power saws are cranked up, the logging trucks are running, continuously, up and down the road, and the aesthetic communal qualities of this valley are altered irrevocably forever. Like the "twilight of the Gods" in a Wagnerian opera, an era is rapidly coming to an end here in the Canada community, as it is in other development-designated areas of Jackson County. I'm reminded of the words of poets such as Tennyson ("the days that are no more") and Sandburg ("our past—like a bucket of ashes"). My worst fear is that I am seeing the last days of any sort of tranquility or rural innocence here in Tuckasegee, and the mourning period has already begun. Just knowing that I will soon be writing in an unnatural noise-filled environment has already changed my relationship with this place which has given me, up until now, such a period of joy and reprieve. I will miss this place, even as I remain here with my memories and my words.

The End of Eden

At times I think there are no words
But these to tell what's true
And there are no truths outside the Gates of Eden.
— Bob Dylan, "The Gates of Eden"

It's the end of October and I've still got tomatoes on the vine. Native, June-blooming rhododendrons are flowering again. Hummingbirds are still here and coming to the feeders. Walnuts hanging from the leafless walnut trees like Christmas tree ornaments, not able to drop. Yellow-jackets still coming and going actively to their underground nests. Raccoons still coming into the corn patch thinking that August must have come 'round again and that there is corn. Following the wettest summer on record, we're in the midst of a draught. Here in Tuckasegee, it's only rained twice in the last two months. I'm having to hand-water the heather, just to keep them alive. With my woodpile ready for the winter, I've not even thought about starting a fire. Strange days.

Usually an early riser, these days I find I'm getting up later (8:00, 8:30, 9:00, 9:30!). It's as if my subconscious is resisting, not wanting to face the day. I'm usually a hopeful person—searching the darkness for a sign of light. These days, however, my mood is much more often one of resignation. I find that I'm walking about in the world looking for signs of natural beauty while I still can, unsure of how much longer it (Nature) or we (the human species) will be around to enjoy it. What this is all about is that the weather, usually an after-thought in the news, is now-a-days the lead story. Flooding. Hurricanes. Earthquakes. Tornadoes. Tsunamis. Draught. Global warming. In addition to all the weather news, there are stories of pandemics, greedy politicians, oil mongers, corporate raiders and mindless terrorism. I'm reminded of a true story I heard about twenty-five years ago told by a Sufi teacher—about a meeting that he had had with his guru. When visiting India during the 1950s at the height of nuclear escalation and conflict between Russia and the United States, and sitting at the feet of this wise and gray-bearded man, he asked the question: "What is going to happen to us, to everything?" After a long pause the elderly prophet turned to the young Sufi novitiate and said, "It's not what you think." "Do you mean that there is not going to be a nuclear war or some sort of nuclear holocaust," the younger man responded. Again there was a long pause, until finally the old man looked the younger in the eye and said: "Mass insanity." To me, this true story seems to sum up and explain almost everything we are experiencing these days. The idea of moderation seems to have been thrown out with both the baby and the bathwater. Everything man-made is being conceived of and is being done in excess. Consequently, it's as if the Earth woke up one day this year, took a look at what was going on around her, and shouted, "I'm mad as hell, and I'm not going to take it any more!"

The end-of-the-world cartoons that appear regularly in the printed media are beginning to look more and more pragmatic. Prophetic. If one looks at the data offered up by the scientific community having to do with economics, ozone and CO_2 pollution, population, etc., the arc of all graphs converge around the year 2000 and shoot straight up, skyward, out of sight. In the past two hundred years—following what had previously been millennia of relative environmental stability—instability in the environment has steadily been on the rise, and what we're looking at, now and into the indefinite future, is a dubious lifestyle based on essential maintenance and repair. In fact, what we may be witnessing is the end of Eden.

While what I'm talking about, here, is a global problem with global ramifications, looking at what is going on right around me serves as a good an example as anything anywhere else on earth, and is more the reason for my lethargy and my excessive sleep habits. Excess, surreal wealth and overpopulation have all become my neighbors here in

Tuckasegee. Less than two miles down the road, the Bear Lake Reserve has already sold two hundred lots and has plans, I am told, for five hundred more homes before it is finished. That would bring seven hundred new homes, almost overnight, into a community that is one of the most rural mountain farming communities in western North Carolina. The economic and cultural effects of this development of second and third homes, owned by people (with a median age of 39!) who are primarily from out of state, will be shocking, if not devastating, to the natives and long-time residents of this community.

Even closer to home, the eighty-acre pasture and mountain adjacent to where I live is currently in the hands of its third real estate agent/developer and there are rumors circulating of a shopping center or possibly a rock quarry being built on this land to serve the Bear Lake gated community—to supply gravel for roads or as a convenience to its residents so they wouldn't have to drive to Sylva or Cashiers to shop. Highway 281 that runs in front of my house, is already over-run with traffic. With seven hundred more families and a shopping mart next door, the pasture-pristine bottomlands of the Canada community will soon look and feel more like the Loves Field community at the entrance to Walmart. The relative peacefulness and serenity that has been my life, here, for the past thirteen years, will be replaced by even more heavy equipment and truck noise, not to mention the glaring all-night lights in the shopping mall that will take the place of the stars in the sky. The end of an era. The "End of Eden."

At a recent address given to the Environmental Leadership Council at Warren Wilson College, ninety-one year old ecologian (a title designed especially for him combining the fields of ecology and theology), Thomas Berry told his audience, "We're looking at a new era in Earth history. I call it The Ecozoic period. Ecology will dominate both the news and our consciousness. With combined planetary perils ever-present, we're looking at a new paradigm for humanity. This will mean a new era of activism that will fall predominantly on the shoulders of the younger generation, who will inherit the dubious job of recovery and reinhabitation of our natural habitat—saving what's left of Eden—

manning the social programs that will care for the unexpectedly displaced and destitute at a time when food, health and shelter can no longer be taken for granted."

With a similar message given to an all-to-sparse audience at Western Carolina University in Cullowhee, noted scientist and expert on global climate change William Schlesinger said, "The rising human population, currently at 6.5 billion, has brought about changes in the basic chemistry of earth's atmosphere and oceans, which have formed the evolutionary environment for all life now on Earth. There has been irreparable damage. The arctic ice we are losing, for example, will never be replaced. To ignore climate change and other global environmental problems is fundamentally and ethically wrong."

With experts like these lined up in agreement, the writing is on the wall. The garden-world of the planet Earth is fast disappearing, and being replaced by a noxious environment created from man's disrespect for Nature and his greed for material and personal wealth and would-be comfort. The end of Eden.

If this is true, then what incentive do I have to get up each morning with the sun and go out into the daylight (or in the case of the Smoky Mountains, the smog) to work in my garden, or to gather firewood in the woods, or to throw a trout-line into the Tuckaseigee River across the road? No wonder all I want to do is sleep! Unable, any longer in clear conscience to see the world as one where natural beauty and diversity abound, and where our needs are provided for, dreams, these days, seem a better option. A pity, as once upon a time we had it all—a *Garden of Eden*. This was, before we turned our backs and walked away.

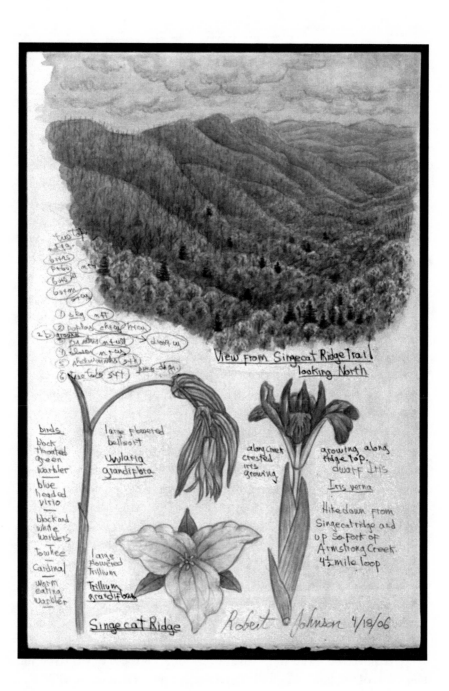

View from Singecat Ridge Trail
looking North

birds
black
throated
green
warbler

blue
headed
vireo

black and
white
warblers

Towhee

Cardinal

worm
eating
warbler

large flowered
bellwort
Uvularia
grandiflora

along creek
crested
iris
growing

growing along
ridge top.
dwarf Iris
Iris verna

Hike down from
Singecat ridge and
up So.Fork of
Armstrong Creek
4½ mile loop

large
flowered
trillium
Trillium
grandiflora

Singecat Ridge

Robert Johnson 4/18/06

93

What Next?

I want to respond, here, to all the many people who have called, written, and spoken to me in person on the streets these past couple weeks since my editorial "The End of Eden" came out. The response has been overwhelming. I'm both humbled and encouraged at the same time. People have expressed to me their displeasure and exasperation regarding the current out-of-control development in Jackson County, and the refrain of these recent conversations has been: "What can we do?" While my earlier assessment of the situation was pretty bleak, let me fall back, here, on the old adage of "better late than never." While most of the large parcels of available land have already been bought up by out-of-state developers (such as the Texas *Centex Corp.*), and the landscape of Jackson County is being altered and dozed into submission as we speak, we don't know what the future holds, or what our efforts, now, will mean down the road.

In my piece "The End of Eden," I was essentially talking about the big picture by giving examples of how things are being impacted locally. The development issue in Jackson County and the Bear Lake Reserve development are really only symptoms of a larger virus that is plaguing our country, and in fact, our world. In truth, we are living in dark times. I think in the future, people will look back on *these* days and the days to come and will refer to them as "The Dark Ages." The real essence of my editorial was about the need for us to begin discussing taboo topics, such as overpopulation, global warming, free-trade capitalism. These are the true issues that are at the heart of what's wrong in the world. Everything else is just a symptom of these greater "illnesses."

I've never believed in the idea of "evil." But these days, given the behavior of certain people in government in Washington DC, I'm beginning to rethink my previous position. What I used to see as misguided behavior, more and more, seems to be down-right destructive, and, yes, even evil. In bleak times like these in which we are living, what, then, can we do? To that imposing question, all I can do is to share with you the epiphany I had the other night while eating supper and listening to the evening news. In the midst of a string of depressing stories on Iraq, global warming, the collapse of GM, the privatization of public lands, and corporate raiding, a single thought came to me— Flood the collective human consciousness and senses with all the beauty we can muster! Music, voice, language, literature, architecture, art, advertising, product design... Everything seen and heard. The shadow world of ignorance and greed, while a powerful one, has no defense against beauty. Of this I am convinced. We don't need to fight fire with fire, or respond in kind to the ways of the wicked and the monetarily possessed. If we just flood the marketplaces, the pages of our papers, the air waves, the museums, the theatres, the shops, the streets, and our minds with beauty, I believe we'll have a chance to turn things around. It's a subtle, if not radical approach. But it just may be worth a try.

While this may seem to some a little far-fetched, it's the best idea I've had lately in terms of coming up with some solutions to the issues I brought up in my "Eden" editorial. While my focus, here, is global, this doesn't mean that there isn't work to be done locally, in terms of encouraging the right people to run for County and City offices in terms of discussing, rationally, the alternatives provided by adopting certain zoning ordinances, and in continuing to support and work with grassroots organizations such as the Canary Coalition and other groups working to protect the air quality in western North Carolina, as well as working to improve education and coming to grips with the problems with our roads. But while acting locally, we must continue to think globally, for what is happening to the rest of the world affects us all, just as what is happening here in Jackson County affects the rest of the world.

King Kong
as a Metaphor for Today

Several weeks ago I wrote an editorial letter focusing on the idea of the "end of Eden." In this letter, I discussed environmental and cultural issues here in the western North Carolina mountains. There was an enormous amount of response to this letter and its fairly depressing scenario of the future of home and habitat here in our region.

In order to temper responses from people who wanted to see the positive side of the coin and to hear what we (the year-round residents) could do to try to turn things around, I wrote a second Letter to the Editor a couple of weeks later, wherein I proposed, as an antidote to uncontrolled development and the inherent greed and lack of environmental consciousness of the corporations fanning the flames of "progress," that we flood the human senses and psyche with beauty. I was told prior to the publication of the second letter that my idea was too abstract, too poetic, and that people may not understand what I was getting at. I really couldn't imagine that anyone would have problems with something as simple and concrete as the notion of "beauty." We all know what beauty is, right? Apparently not, as the response I received to my second letter was the complete opposite from what I experienced with the "End of Eden" piece. What I got this time was a total lack of response. Not one e-mail. Not one letter. Not one phone call. No one stopping me on the street. Nothing.

Apparently people really didn't get the "beauty thing." Ok. So this time let's try it this way: Go see *KING KONG*! I'm serious. Yes, the film *King Kong* that's currently playing in theatres all over the Western NC region. At the core of this recent remake of the old Hollywood classic, is the French story of *Beauty & The Beast*. The last lines spoken in the current remake are: "It wasn't the airplanes, it was beauty killed the beast." In my previous letter to the editor I wrote "We don't need to fight fire with fire, or respond in kind to the ways of the wicked and the monetarily possessed." In that sense, we don't need airplanes and military firepower, nor do we need big bank accounts, to stave off the bestial onslaught of developers and the energy conglomerates with government officials in their pockets. We can use beauty to "kill" the beast. If the idea of beauty is a baffling one to you in this context, then go see the film. It's all there. The greedy capitalistic drive of the Hollywood film-maker. The glittering diamonds of the New York theatre-goers who pay big bucks to see for themselves "Kong: The Eighth Wonder of the World." And, most importantly, the dynamic of the film's heroine and the giant ape, i.e., the way that beauty "conquers" the beast. Let the film-maker be a metaphor for the out-of-state conglomerate developers. Let the diamond-laden theatre-goers be the out-of-state land owners of high-end lots and second homes in gated communities. Let the film's heroine Naomi Watts be "beauty," and let King Kong be "the beast," representing the military-industrial complex and its henchmen in Washington DC. Take particular notice of how, when Kong is deprived of beauty, or when beauty is threatened, he goes into destroy-mode, laying waste to New York City. Compare this to the idea of how clear-cutting our forests or over-populating our mountains and mountain-tops with homes "lays waste" to the natural beauty of that place, and can easily destroy resources such as water, soil, and wildlife from erosion and toxic run-off.

In the film Naomi Watts (beauty) tames King Kong (the beast). In the same way, I believe, by flooding the marketplace, the pages of our papers, the airwaves, the museums, the theaters, the shops, the streets and our minds and language with beauty, we, too, can "tame" the more primitive and self-indulgent urges of the beast of progress and ownership. We can, in fact, turn things around.

The North Carolina Land Rush

In recent days, the comparison of western North Carolina to the rush for gold mining in California during the 19th century keeps coming to mind. As I see the high-end housing developments going up, and as I read this Sunday's *Asheville Citizen-Times* article on the Bush proposal to sell off parcels of National Forest land, I'm thinking "gold rush!" Just as settlers and entrepreneurs from all over the country rushed to California during the 1840s and 1850s following the cry of "there's gold in them there hills!", the get-rich-quick mentality and the pandemic of the recent real estate boom we're experiencing in this part of the country, now, has become more than pervasive. New agents and developers are appearing here in the mountains to stake their claims and are buying up all the land their deep pockets can hold. Instead of gold, the developers are, in fact, mining for land. ("There's *land* in them there hills!") They're scouring the hills of the state's most rugged (and ironically, most vulnerable) western counties for land upon which they can put their gated communities full of extravagant million-dollar homes—homes that are popping up on the local landscape like pimples on the face of a pubescent teen-age boy. This simile is not lost on many residents I have spoken to over the past few months. Such is the "acne" upon the natural "flesh" of these hills many of us lovingly look upon and caress as we farm, hike, hunt and fish the hills and hollers that we call home.

As I say, I'm not the only one who feels that we've been invaded by armies of interlopers from the outside, and that the look and feel of our mountains has undergone a hideous "make-over." I'm hearing similar sentiments from across the board in our community—from scientists, local farmers, academicians, blacksmiths, shopkeepers, home builders, natives, recent residents, and others. Many of us are beginning to feel the pressure of overpopulation and developmental overkill. It's like we're getting pushed out of our habitat by a kind of human tsunami that has rolled into these mountains like a great tidal wave.

Don't get me wrong. I'm not complaining about those people who have been coming to these mountains all their lives and have decided to bring their families here to live permanently. These people, for the most part, have come to love the mountains and have, over time, learned and accepted the geographic and cultural nature of the place. What I'm railing about, here, is the increasing number of people from the outside who spend only a few weeks, or at most a few months here, and who could care less about the local culture and customs, or who they are pushing out of their homes because of their oversized bank accounts and suburban mansions that inflate both the local economy as well as land taxes.

That said, the recent news of the federal government's proposal to sell off numerous tracts of National Forest land in these mountains, is the last straw, the final insult, and is a true wake-up call for everyone with a willing voice to stand up and be counted, lest we lose everything under our feet, including the soil.

As I say, there are many people who have expressed their concern in writing or vocally about the "gold rush" mentality that has invaded our mountains, and which threatens to disfigure them and to displace us in the process. I sincerely hope that others will also pick up the standard and will begin to speak up, get involved in this controversy, and stand up and be counted for what they believe is truly best for this place and its people.

Playing With Paradox
Using Development to Save Mountain Farms
(A Conversation)

In the decades since World War II the farms of Henry County, Kentucky, have become increasingly mechanized. Though they are still comparatively diversified, they are less diversified than they used to be. The holdings are larger, the owners are fewer.

The land is falling more and more into the hands of speculators and professional people from the cities, who—in spite of all the scientific agricultural miracles—still have much more money than farmers. Because of big technology and big economics, there is more abandoned land in the county than ever before. Many of the better farms are visibly deteriorating, for want of manpower and time and money to maintain them properly."

— Wendell Berry, *The Unsettling of America*

On Thursday of last week, at an unlikely meeting of the minds, Sylva developer John Beckman and Whittier farmer William Shelton sat down at a long table in the back of the Spring Street Café in Sylva, over maps and blueprints, to talk about the issue of disappearing farmland here in the mountains of western North Carolina. Beckman, before investing in real estate in the county in 1993 and moving to Jackson County full time in 2000, was in real estate and historic building preservation in the Triangle area of Raleigh/Durham/Chapel Hill, and was a past President of the Carolina Farm Stewardship Association (Mountain Chapter), as well as a member of the Triangle Land Conservancy and the American Farmland Trust. William Shelton, on the other hand, was born and raised in Jackson County and went to study Agricultural Science at the University of Tennessee before returning to his

100

family farm in Whittier, where he has been crop-farming tomatoes, strawberries, lettuce and market vegetables full-time for the past twenty-two years.

With the kind of explosive economic growth the country has experienced over the last decade, and the sky-rocketing rise of real estate development in western North Carolina, the issue of the growing scarcity of family farms and mountain farmland has become a real issue, with increasing pressure to develop the limited farmland in our region due to its flatland accessibility and site preparation advantages. I had arranged for Shelton and Beckman to come together, on this day, to try and find common ground in terms of how their individual professions might benefit one another and to find the basis for some sort of sustainable model for other developers and farmers for the future with respect to balancing land development with environmental protection and farmland preservation.

After discussing the county's current political climate and parallel issues such as land-use planning, steep slope ordinances and sediment control legislation, which have been the subject of much discussion in recent months throughout the mountain region, the conversation turned to the issue at hand.

"I've been reading a book titled *Collapse*," offers Shelton, "which has a chapter about what is going on, now, out in the state of Montana. This is something I know something about, as I've been going to Montana, to fish, for some time, now. The picture that the author paints in this book on the collapse of farmlands and the environment at the hands of industry and housing development, is almost an exact mirror of what we are, at present, experiencing here in western North Carolina. Unless we take progressive action, now, in terms of legislation, preservation and education, the full-time residents of Jackson County and its neighboring counties will be looking at a grim picture where the future is concerned. Land along this bottom where I farm, that not all that long ago was selling for $300 to $500 an acre, is now selling for as much as $100,000 an acre. Flat bottom land is choice real estate here in the mountains, and the prices are only going to rise as out-of-state developers come in here looking for choice sites for their gated communities, retirement and second homes. Why, they're selling property up in Tuckasegee from helicopters, with buyers not even setting foot on the ground! $300,000 for ⅓-acre lots. With this kind of development, land values are escalating exponentially, and land taxes are becoming so inflated that it's harder and harder for local people and small family farmers, like myself, to make ends meet. People around here who have farmed for generations are being forced to sell out. This is not only a change in the culture of the community, but a blow to the availability of local food, which effects everyone."

With the ball, now, clearly in his court, John Beckman was quick to respond. "I agree that the loss of American farmland to economic pressures and development has reached a precarious point in our history, and that it has become increasingly difficult for the small family farms to remain operationally productive and keep their heads above the rising dangerous waters of American agricultural policies, practices and realities. It seems to me that farmers may need to diversify not only their crops and conventional practices, but the very design and use of their lands, if their farms are to remain in their hands as sustainable, productive ground. I'd like to suggest, as something of a solution, that it's time for farmers to get their slice of the development pie and integrate it into their farm plan as a working asset, instead of falling back on the old pattern of a last-ditch sellout to developers. Combining farmlands with development may sound like an oxymoron, but it could prove to be a most useful tool for keeping farm families on the farm."

When William Shelton asks Beckman just how this plan of his would play out and what his formula for implementation would be, Beckman answered by saying that as a businessman he is interested in finding threatened tracts of farmland and wild acreage and coming up with a kind of formula to protect a large portion of them. Interested in protecting watersheds, as well as bottom farmland, he suggested that his process would be to first identify what the key areas or properties are that need to be protected and then seek to protect productive farmland by designating specific development areas and a thoughtful list of regulations governing how that development takes place. Emphasis, he said, would be on minimizing the impacts on the land and water resources and keeping prime farmland in crops, not driveways.

"Most folks who run Mom-and-Pop businesses here in the mountains where we live, have a 'retirement plot' set aside to sell and support themselves in old age," says Shelton. "The farmer, on the other hand, lives in and on his business. So when it comes time to retire, he has to sell the whole farm. Farmers aren't especially known for investing in retirement options across the period of a lifetime. This being the case, how, then, does your plan benefit the farmers? Could you be more specific about this plan for a progressive development paradigm?"

"I want to put the farmer in the developer's seat," Beckman answers, confidently. "In other words, the farmer becomes the developer. The design I have in mind and have been promoting is a holistic approach with an emphasis placed on protecting the land and its productive potential. This type of design has been called by others, 'Conservation-based Community Design.' This design system takes the best farmlands, saves those, and develops around the farmland on unusable areas and sets the rest of the property in conservation and/or preservation easements. Specifically, the development design I have in mind reflects three essential criteria: (1) to provide for long-term protection of the natural beauty, bio-diversity, and ecosystems present on the property, (2) to develop sustainable business and agricultural opportunities that support the needs and enjoyment of the residents, and (3) to create a small community atmosphere offering enriching, social, educational, and recreational opportunities for residents and visitors."

"This all sounds very generous, but what do you, as a developer have to gain from this scenario," asks Shelton.

"I have come up with a formula that works for me. Financially, it works out to a near zero-sum gain. I just want to get the bulk of my investment back and to have it available for additional preservation projects. And I'm willing to work on this basis," says Beckman. "I've just bought 190 acres over on Tilley Creek—the site of the Shooting Range controversy. I'm planning on selling six lots for home-sites, the rest will go into conservation and the bottom will remain in farmland along the creek. If I set the price for the lots slightly above the going price, I should be able to get most of my investment back. Meanwhile, I've preserved valuable local farmland and set about 120 acres in conservation. This, in essence, is my model and my formula. It's not about huge profits, it's about recouping your investment and saving large tracts of tillable bottomland, as well as a large percentage of the watershed, and then moving on to the next piece of land that is crying out for preservation. "

"I see what you're getting at, here," says Shelton. "But local people won't be able to afford to buy land at these kinds of prices. How does this help local people and their need for affordable, even low-income housing?"

Beckman: "Yes, the pitfall of my projected program is that it's going to cost a quarter million dollars for a house-site—which often means bringing in wealthy people from the outside. This scenario has, up until now, been part of the problem. So, admittedly, my scenario doesn't account for these particular community needs you're speaking about. Where we succeed in preserving valuable land, we fail to provide low-cost home-sites. Additional programs need to be developed that specifically address this issue."

Shelton: "We're in a race against time, in Jackson County, right now. Ours is a unique scenario. I looks to me like there needs to be some kind of county involvement, then, if this farmland preservation plan of yours is going to work. We're going to need several "tools"— accessible and yet comprehensive tools when looking at the overall picture. What I see is some kind of partnership between the county, land trusts, real estate investors and private individuals and groups working together with the betterment of the county in mind."

Beckman: "Yes, you're right. We'll need to create public/private partnerships as working models. As farmer-developers we'll have to work with land trusts and county governments for this scenario to succeed."

Shelton: "This is a very unselfish design concept. You're a developer. Developers are known for their profit incentives. What's given you the incentive to come up with this preservation concept and to actually put it into practice here in Jackson County?"

Beckman: "I've been working on farms since I was four years old. It started with my grandfather teaching me how to plant peas. More recently I've been growing truck gardens and selling produce to local families, farmers markets and local businesses. I've become attached to my new geographical home in Jackson County and my adopted community, and want to see it survive this latest historical assault on it's integrity. In terms of incentives, if not me, then who will be willing to be an advocate for farmland preservation? These big out-of-state developers aren't going to step up, and farmers have rarely been able to satisfactorily organize to protect themselves. I see America making huge mistakes in terms of farmland policy. And I think that we, here in the mountains, need more local food sources. Keeping local farms intact promotes food security, reduces transportation costs and fuel consumption, preserves rural landscapes and encourages good environmental stewardship."

Shelton: "My best guess is that we're going to need local food in the future. With no farmland or farmers left, who's going to provide local foods? In terms of the kind of partnerships we've been talking about, I can envision local farmers working with the county in terms of supplying produce to school food programs, Meals on Wheels, and other county-supported food services. Better quality food for less money, which is a win for the local farmer and a win for all these services and their recipients."

Beckman: "In this country at the moment, it all comes down to the bottom line. In a capitalistic society, money is king. The challenge is, how to inject values into a system without ethical values. Cash is like fish. You gotta keep it moving or it goes bad. My feeling is, why not use it in a positive and progressive way? By having a farm at the center of a development, residents and visitors can't help but become connected with the importance of food and fiber production at the local level. My hope is that the current trend in interest regarding organic foods could carry over into the farmland real estate market and into the consciousness of potentially enlightened developers and buyers— creating a fad or trend for future farmland preservation.

"There's a lot of good information available about sustainable farming practices and improving soil health, but this concept of 'farm development planning' seems to have been overlooked as a management option. I'm hoping that our efforts here, today, will be a beginning that will encourage other farmers to diversify their farm plans with strategies that succeed in keeping their farms in joyful, sustainable, production."

Shelton: "Yes, and it would be great to see a marriage between local markets and producers. This would take a lot of stress out of the marketing side of my business and be, ultimately, more rewarding. And then, I could lease my farm to new, young farmers—when I'm ready to retire."

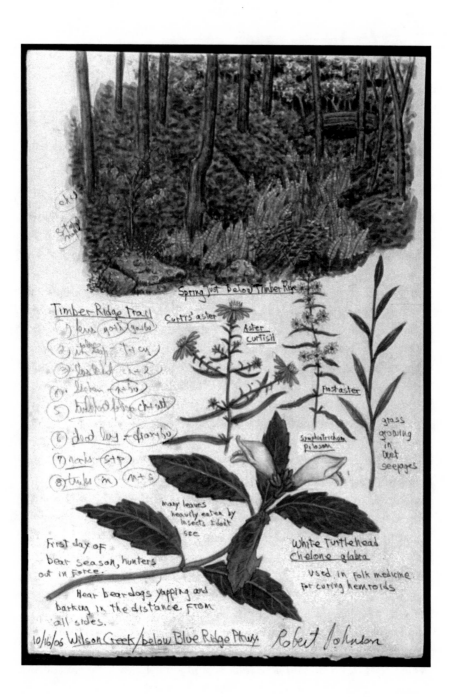

107

The Blue Wall

Jewel of the Blue Ridge Escarpment
Goes Up For Sale

I have lived since 1984 in the eastern end of Jackson County, North Carolina, on the plateau of the Southern Appalachians known as the Blue Ridge Escarpment, or what was known to the Cherokee as "The Blue Wall." This geologic wonder of 150,000 acres of sheer wall cliffs and gorges, stretches eastward from the west fork of the Chattooga River in northeast Georgia and runs some sixty miles along the North Carolina, South Carolina state line past the Greenville watershed. My forays in the Nantahala National Forest have taken me into the Escarpment to places like the Horsepasture and Toxaway Rivers, Whiteside Mountain and the headwaters of the Chatooga and into the Pisgah National Forest side of the Escarpment on fishing, canoeing and hiking trips as well as my work with Cherokee elders to identify and protect cultural and religious sites.

In my opinion, this "eastern wall" of the Southern Appalachians is some of the most exciting and beautiful country in all of the Blue Ridge. An area of dramatic range—from 1,000 foot rock faces to high mountain balds, and from dynamic waterfalls to peaceful finger-lakes, the Blue Wall/Blue Ridge Escarpment, as photographer/conservation activist Thomas Wyche says, is truly one of the world's great wilderness areas.

Right in the middle of the Blue Ridge Escarpment (which includes the Chattahooche National Forest, Sumter National Forest, Nantahala National Forest, Ellicot Rock Wilderness, Table Rock State Park, the Mountain Bridge Wilderness, Table Rock Watershed, and Poinsett Watershed) lies a 50,000 acre tract surrounding Lake Jocassee and the Jocassee Gorge area owned by the Duke Power Company. And herein lies the essence of this story.

The conservation arm of the Duke Power Company has decided to sell this 50,000 acre keystone area of The Blue Wall. In doing so, they have given first option to key governmental and independent conservation groups (South Carolina Department of Natural Resources, the Heritage Trust Program, and the Nature Conservancy in particular) hoping that these preservation organizations can come up with the necessary capital to buy the land, thus consolidating the entire Blue Wall region, and consequently securing its status as protected wilderness, indefinitely.

In an effort to bring the issue of the purchase of this land area to public attention, photographer Thomas Wyche and the South Carolina Chapter of the Nature Conservancy have teamed up and taken this unprecedented opportunity to the streets. In a public presentation held at Greenville, South Carolina's Peace Center, a Thomas Wyche/James Kilgo/Westcliffe Publishers book *The Blue Wall: Wilderness of the Carolinas and Georgia* was launched and put on sale, with all proceeds going to the Nature Conservancy of South Carolina to aide in raising money toward the incremental purchase of portions of the Duke Power tract. The evening included state and local dignitaries, Greenville-area patrons, and conservationists from every arm of the regional community. Wyche, the photographer, and Kilgo, the writer, gave engaging intimate accounts of their associations with and concerns for the preservation of this unique bit of our Southern Appalachian bioregion. Their reading and photographic slide presentation was received with standing ovations from a near capacity crowd. Hundreds of copies of the beautiful coffee-table-size book were sold and the announcement was made by the Nature Conservancy that the first purchase of 1,000 acres on the east side of Lake Jocassee along the Laurel Fork Creek drainage had been made by the Heritage Trust Fund just that morning—initiating the process of purchase toward the eventual goal of accumulating all of the 50,000 acres of the Duke Power tract.

So, what does all this mean to the average resident of western North Carolina and the Southern Appalachians? The Lake Jocassee Gorge watershed, by all objective accounts is one of the most unique and beautiful wilderness areas in the whole of the United States. It is home to re-introduction programs for the peregrine falcon, golden eagle, wild turkey and red fox. It is a protected black bear habitat. It is home to bobcat, deer and native trout. It is one of the world's richest bio-diverse ecosystems, providing nurturance to a very large, rich and healthy indigenous plant community. It is an area replete with awe-inspiring topography: turbulent rivers, laurel-lined gorges, pristine lakes, poetic waterfalls, flower-populated glens....

Consider, for instance, that within this thirty mile Duke Power tract of The Blue Wall there are—

1. two of only four National Wild and Scenic Rivers in the south-eastern United States (the Chattooga, and Horsepasture)
2. five deep gorges containing the racing waters of the Whitewater, Thompson, Bearcamp, Horsepasture and Toxaway Rivers, as well as another smaller gorge containing the Eastatoe River and a South Carolina Trust Reserve
3. some of the most spectacular waterfalls in the eastern United States (Windy Falls on the Horsepasture, the remote Thompson River Falls, Bearwallow and Bearcamp Creek Falls and Toxaway Creek Falls—perhaps the longest cascade of falls in the East)
4. nine thousand acres of the Ellicot's Rock Wilderness Area with its joint boundaries of Georgia, South Carolina and North Carolina; five South Carolina State Parks (Devil's Fork, Oconee, Keowee, Toxaway, Jones Gap and Caesar's Head)
5. a massive expanse of forested peaks and river gorges comprising one of the largest and most varied headwater ecosystems in the eastern U.S., an area varied enough in climate, orientation, altitude and soils to maintain an incredible variety of plant life
6. last, but not least, Lake Jocassee itself, which photographer Tomas Wyche calls "the turquoise jewel of the Blue Wall."

In short, the Duke Power-owned section of the Blue Ridge Escarpment is both a wilderness and a recreation paradise—streams and lakes for fishermen, waterways for canoeists and kayakers, thousands of acres of deciduous and evergreen forests full of birds and indigenous plant life for birdwatchers and wildflower lovers, and all of the above for the diverse and prolific animal life that, let's not forget, has equal rights to live and play here, too.

The Duke Power–Lake Jocassee–Blue Wall–Blue Ridge Escarpment area up for sale is of importance and benefit, therefore, to everyone living in and around these Southern Blue Ridge Mountains. And for all the reasons mentioned above, and more, this area is of vital concern to us all who call this region "home." Not only for us, but for our children and their children it is important that this final link in the chain of the larger 154,000 acre area containing all of the Blue Ridge Escarpment be secured and protected from the hands of uncontrolled private and commercial development. Which will surely and inevitably occur should such conservation groups as the Nature Conservancy, the Heritage Trust, and other local and regional preservation-minded groups come up short in their efforts to raise money for the purchase of this land. While Duke Power has, commendably, extended its hand to these conservation and preservation groups, giving them a first and unchallenged chance at the purchase of the 50,000 acres Lake Jocassee Gorge tract, they have not, in any way, offered any portion of this land as a gift to the public they purport to be so in league with. Rather, they have been very clear concerning the conditions of their proposal for the conservation groups of the region—conditions which include an all-business, definitive deadline, as well as a promise to place this 50,000 acre tract on the commercial market and open to the highest bidder after the window of opportunity for conservation groups has elapsed.

Given the relatively short period of grace from Duke Power and the size of the area being sold, in order for this area to be purchased and enshrined as a protected wilderness area, we all need to get involved, lest this magnificent land be lost to us forever as a place we can experience and use as our own. This means talking to friends and neighbors; calling the Nature Conservancy or local conservation groups for more detailed and specific information regarding tax-deductible contributions, assistance, etc.; using our imagination—organizing local benefits, raffles, and cake walks; visiting the Lake Jocassee Gorge watershed to experience, first hand, the splendor of the region; buying *The Blue Wall* book, which is a true family keepsake of the region). Saving the Lake

Jocassee tract is not something that the government and the moneyed conservation patrons are going to be able to do on their own. For this area to be secured by the declared Duke Power deadline, all of us need to get involved. If this precious tract of wilderness slips through our hands as the result of inaction and apathy, it will be gone forever. Given over to the gluttony of roads, condominiums, logging interests and lumber mills, hundreds of private homeowners and everything that comes with the unconscious hollow-bellied hunger of unchecked capitalism and progress. Gone will be the quiet, glass-like surfaces for my canoe to glide across the finger-lakes of Jocassee. Gone, the intimate fishing trips along the Horsepasture and Whitewater. Gone, the silent stillness of the woods, looking for wildflowers and morel mushrooms in the spring. Gone, the psychic security of simply knowing that not all of this continent has been over-run with the plague of over-population.

As conservationist singer-songwriter Woody Guthrie wrote in the first half of the century during his bohemian travels across this continent of ours: "This land is your land, this land is my land, from the Gulf Stream waters to the New York island, this land is made for you and me." With these song-lines as our banner and this perception as our cause, the Duke Power tract of the The Blue Wall can be, and will be, protected from progress forever. Having grown up in Graham County, NC near the Joyce Kilmer National Forest, and in Raybun County, GA with the Nantahala National Forest just out my back door, I think of the Lake Jocassee Gorge area also as part of that big backyard. The back forty of my boyhood, the woodlot of my old age.... This land is my land. But this land is also your land. And I hope to see you there in years to come—on the mirror-like turquoise water of the Jocassee, in hip-boots with rod wading the Horsepasture or along the trail.

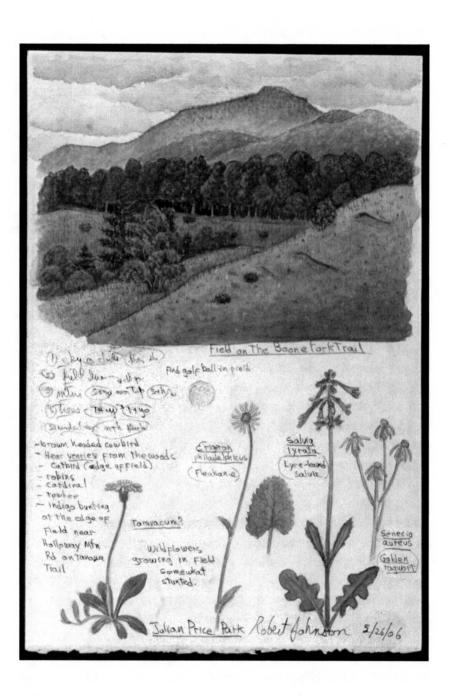

Field on the Boone Fork Trail

① sky in clouds (the sky)
② field (see valley)
③ mtns (say on top) (Satis)
④ trees (Treey) ? ? ? yo
⑤ bundel of mtn shrubs

- brown headed cowbird
- hear veeries from the woods
- Catbird (edge of field)
- robins
- cardinal
- towhee
- indigo bunting
  at the edge of
  field near
  Holloway Mtn
  Rd on Tanawa
  Trail

Find golf ball in field

Erigeron philadelphicus (Fleabane)

Salvia lyrata (Lyre-leaved salvia)

Senecio aureus (Golden ragwort)

Taraxacum?

Wildflowers growing in field somewhat stunted.

Julian Price Park   Robert Johnson   5/26/06

113

Stacking the Deck

The following editorial is an excerpt of a longer article which appeared in the author's hometown newspaper during the pre-election campaign period for a new Board of County Commissioners in 2006. As a direct result of this article, no less than two of the pro-development candidates running for political office were eliminated from the race, and a pro-land-use-regulations Jackson County native was elected to office in their place.

L ike good news, bad news also travels fast. It has come to my attention this week that there are at least three candidates running for the Jackson County Board of Commissioners who either work for or have direct or closely indirect connections with major large-acreage, gated, sub-division developments in Jackson County. If this is true, one begins to wonder what, in fact, is going on here? If this is true, it brings up certain issues which have broad-ranging implications for all of us here in this county.

With the Chair of the Board of County Commissioners running unopposed, as someone who has publicly revealed his connections to Balsam Mountain Preserve, one has to wonder if there is some kind of "conspiracy" afoot to stack the deck on the Board with people who are pro-development. This would certainly, from an outsider's perspective, seem to be the case. Common sense logic and simple math will get you to this conclusion very fast, if you look at the players and look at their connections to large-scale development and to each other.

A Board of Commissioners made up largely of people with vested interests and who are in the pocket of corporate developers doesn't bode well for the future of our county. There are many examples, here in the South, as well as in other parts of the country, where the big out-of-state developers have come into rural communities and essentially bought up all the available large tracts of land, built their gated communities of million-dollar homes, then stacked the deck on the local Board of Commissioners, allowing them to have their way, financially, politically and culturally, with the future of those places. We, here in Jackson County are facing a similar plight, if we don't stand up and take notice, and cast our votes in the upcoming primary elections for either local candidates or candidates who have the welfare of local landowners and citizens at heart, if we sit back on our haunches, unawares, and let these kinds of developers come in, take over, and then invite all their "friends" to come and partake of the wealth of beautiful mountain land, here in our county, we're going to end up as merely a suburb of Cashiers and Highlands, with high land assessment values and taxes to match.

Now is the time to take stock of who the candidates are in this election and what their connections are to big business and large development, and/or where they stand on the issues pertaining to land-use and land-use regulations (such as steep-slope and ridge-top ordinances, as well as sediment control regulations, etc.). From where I sit, out in Tuckasegee—with Centex (a Texas-based company and owners of Bear Lake Reserve) and Legasus Corporation (from Florida) owning several thousand acres of land surrounding our community, and threatening to not only drive locals off their land due to escalating land values, but to build asphalt plants and rock quarries to supply developers with their road-building materials, we need to know who is representing us in local government, and to make sure that the Board is not stacked with employees and sympathizers of the powers that would come into our community and have their way with the land and its people.

Ask Not What Your County
Can Do For You

A sk not what your county can do for you, but what you can do for your county. These familiar (albeit slightly altered) words from former President John F. Kennedy are exactly on target for our current situation here in Jackson County.

As our recently elected county commissioners get on with the business of honoring their pledges to initiate land-use planning, they'll need our support and help to overcome the aggressive resistance and attacks from developers and real-estate brokers who seem to care only about extracting the maximum benefit for themselves at the expense of the rest of us.

In recent days, a few zealous real-estate barons from the Cashiers/Highlands area have made a concerted effort to foment an insurgency based on half-truths and outright lies in order to derail the proposed moratorium on new subdivision development and to halt work on land-use rules. These people have spent thousands of dollars running full-page ads in local papers, radio ads and road signage trying to incite their neighbors to mutiny, to abandon the good ship Jackson County with the subdivision-regulations voyage only just under way. But we, the loyal crew, aren't fooled by their tawdry tactics. Nor are we sympathetic to their in-house studies or their unfounded claims about job losses and a looming economic tsunami. (In fact, the descriptions I've heard concerning similar situations in other states and countries seem to indicate just the opposite — that putting land-use rules in place actually creates jobs by attracting people and businesses to the area.)

In reality, all this amounts to little more than sour grapes. These guys have had their way in Jackson County for so long—selling land with no restrictions of any kind—that they are, in a sense, throwing a tantrum over any attempt, however moderate, to limit business as usual. With only short-term dollar signs in their eyes, they show no concern for either the future or the general welfare of the year-round, working residents of Jackson County.

These same real-estate "professionals" have publicly criticized our commissioners for not conducting a study of the economic impact of a moratorium on the community. It occurs to me that these folks have made no non-partisan study either—but that hasn't stopped them from declaring that a moratorium will result in lost jobs, lost property rights, higher taxes and bringing our local economy to a halt. Where do they get their figures to support such preposterous claims? Where's the beef?

If that weren't enough, It's rumored that some local real-estate agents, developers and construction companies have gone so far as to lay people off and halt construction on certain projects so they could stand up at the Feb. 27 public hearing and the March 8 Commissioners Meeting and proclaim that the economic downward spiral had already begun. If there's any truth to these charges, then these folks have clearly gone over the top, and one can only imagine what they might do next.

Let's not forget that all four commissioners elected in November ran on platforms that endorsed land-use rules for the county. The election results gave those commissioners a clear mandate to provide a balance to the kind of hyper-aggressive development that has invaded Jackson County along with many other parts of Western North Carolina. So it should come as no surprise to anyone that upon taking office, this group and their team of county officials got right to work trying to make good on their promises and save our county from certain ruin at the hands of unchecked development. Yet moratorium opponents are acting as if Jackson County had just been given a pig in a poke.

In the end, this is an economic issue, not a political one. It's not about Democrats or Republicans, and it's not about the loss of jobs. It's about class. It's about the haves and the have-nots, the moneyed elite versus the working and middle classes.

At the moment, the latter two groups outnumber the rich in Jackson County. But that could change if the real-estate folks and the developers have their way. Don't let the expensive ads or the underhanded scare tactics of a few self-serving realtor/developers fool you. They are not the majority, and they don't have your best interests at heart.

But they are making noise, and the rest of us need to do whatever we can to back up our newly elected leaders. We can start by contacting them and voicing our support, writing letters to our local papers, and speaking up at open meetings. We have waited much too long for this day to come, and it's finally here. Jackson County is leading the way toward responsible development in western North Carolina.

So ask not what your county can do for you; ask what you can do for your county.

The Idiot's Wind
a long haiku, for Steve Earle

"Idiot wind...blowing down the back roads headin' south...
It's a wonder that you still know how to breathe."
— Bob Dylan, "Idiot Wind" from *Blood on the Tracks*

Is this the best we can do?
Turn wonderful air
into a hurricane of haze —
Turn landscape and vistas
into pictures painted for the blind —
Fill pink lungs of children
with black space —
Make soot we breathe
surreal salt in the food of film noir,
for profit and at any price.

Is this the best we can do?
From a pile of coal
make heat —
Make light
from a hill of peat —
Like mad midwives
who at birth make the switch —
From hell-bent to heartache
hookers of energy in bed with the rich;
the blood of the poet in a Blue Ridge ditch,
for profit and at any price.

Is this the best we can do?
Stay cool in the face of fire —
The gift of mankind:
an eternal pyre —
Using the mind
as a political gyre,
for profit and at any price.

     Hands and head in a vice.
     Denying Nature not two times, but thrice.
     Fanning the flames of dry ice.
     Use poison in food and calling it spice.
     For what profit? What price?

Is this the best we can do?
Take transfusions of blood in the air —
Honor madmen and government not really there,
who call the rain "sunshine" and the circle square,
for profit and at any price.

Is this the best we can do?
Only an idiot
would try to make love to the wind.
Would inhale oxygen and call it CO2.
Or think sun and moon
would come from some Yahweh living in another place.
Would kiss the lips of bombs and call them sweet.
Or move their home to somewhere in outer space.
This   is grace?
This   the human race?

We can do better than this.

III

TALES FROM THE TAILGATE MARKET

Columns

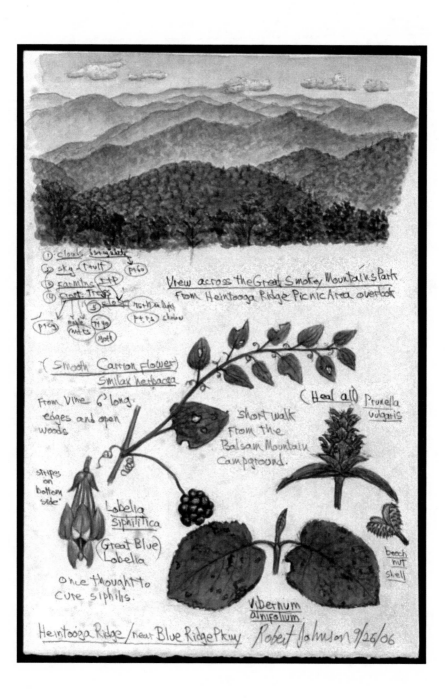

View across the Great Smoky Mountains Park
From Heintooga Ridge Picnic Area overlook

(Smooth Carrion Flower)
Smilax herbacea

From vine 6' long.
edges and open
woods

Short walk
From the
Balsam Mountain
Campground.

(Heal all) Prunella
vulgaris

stripes
on
bottom
side'

Lobelia
siphilitica

(Great Blue)
Lobelia

Once thought to
cure siphilis.

beech
nut
shell

Viburnum
alnifolium

Heintooga Ridge / near Blue Ridge Pkwy   Robert Johnson 9/26/06

123

Ain't Got Nothin' Against Organic Food

It's almost mid-summer and the produce is beginning to come in in bushel baskets instead of in baggies or planted pots. With a near perfect growing season this year, word has gotten out, and here in Jackson County, N.C., folks are getting up early on Saturday morning and making their way to the Jackson County Farmer's Market, where this week there is a bounty of summer squash, new potatoes, Swiss chard, cabbage, lettuce, green beans, onions, carrots, mushrooms, cucumbers, blackberries, and new honey comin' in—not to mention a plethora of native plants, flowers and herbs on hand.

Founded late last season by Karen and Johnny White and Jackson County Agricultural Extension Agent Christine Bredenkamp for local gardeners and growers in Jackson County to have an outlet for sale of their fresh produce, the tailgate market is beginning to pay off. Open on Saturday mornings from 8:00 to 12:00, June through October, the large parking lot off Mill Street behind Peebles Department Store in downtown Sylva is bustling this week with a steady stream of traffic. People are checking things out and buying from a growing number of vendors whose trucks are pulled up with their tailgates hanging over the sidewalk along the side street that parallels the railroad tracks and the town's back street.

With live old-time fiddle music coming from a portable open air tent and the summer sun still somewhat low in the sky, conversation is excited, money is changing hands. People are meeting each other, carrying on conversations started months before, getting to know who's growing what, and the Sylva market is beginning to feel like the social and business center that larger marketplaces all over the world have been for millennia, as growers representing many of the different communities in the county continue to pull in to the large parking lot to unload their goods. Among the regulars there are Ron and Cathy Arps' *Vegenui Gardens* from the Beta community in Sylva, Becky Lipkin's *Becky's Herbs* up in Little Canada, Rick Queen with his hybrid rhododendrons and perennials from John's Creek over in the Caney Fork community, Karen and Johnny White's *Slow Creek Farm* represents East Laporte, Green Barn Nursery from Pumpkintown, Jim Parham and Mary Ellen Hammond's honey from the Almond community, Christine Bredenkamp's Sylva-raised shitake mushrooms, and, of course, yours truly and my *Bobcat Gardens* produce which I have brought in from Tuckasegee.

Most of the grower/vendors here at the Jackson County Farmer's Market are organic growers. For whatever reason, these are the folks who have been showing up to sell their produce for the past month or so. That being the case, it is only natural that conversation would tend to migrate to this topic, as customers and vendors *chaw* about the subject of what is or isn't organic.

It's been a good day for growers and shoppers alike and by the end of the morning the growers are beginning to run short on supply. A large middle-age man in a feed cap that looks a lot like my own has wandered over to my position and is checking out the last few pounds of yellow straight-neck squash that have sunk to the bottom of one of my half-bushel baskets. "This stuff all organic?" he finally asks. "I'm looking for yellow squash, and I see that you've got some here. How much you want for your squash?" "$1.29 a pound," I say. "Same as you'd pay at Ingles, only this ain't grown with all them chemicals and synthetic fertilizers," I respond, trying to mimic his mountain accent and to pitch my produce at the same time. "My grandma used to grow that way—using manure and all for *fertilize*. I can remember all that. Mostly a lot of work, is what I remember. What'll you take for all the rest of your squash?" he asks again. I weight out the remaining squash from the half bushel basket on my scales. "Comes to about $7.09," I say. He comes back at me with, "This organic stuff is high, seems to me." "Same as what you'd pay at the supermarket," I try to say again, with conviction. "Well, I ain't got nothin' against organic vegetables," he goes on, "but it just don't taste the same." "Without all the chemicals and additives," I think, somewhat sarcastically, to myself. "Don't get me wrong, I ain't got nothin' against it, it's just that we've gone beyond all that natural stuff and have got better ways nowadays. The organic stuff just don't taste the same," he says again, and walks away leaving the five-and-a-half pounds of yellow straight-neck squash sitting there in the scales.

About five minutes later a young lady in her late thirties with her young daughter in tow stops at the back of my truck and begins to talk. "I overheard the conversation you were having with that man about organic vegetables. Your squash look beautiful. How is it that we've come to accept the taste—the idea of chemically treated and radiated produce? Oh, it's true that organic vegetables don't taste the same as corporate-grown produce," she says with a slight snicker and a sarcastic gleam in her eye. "Have we become so willing to accept the taste of slow poisons as part of our daily diet? Is there really any question where all the cancer is coming from these days? Look at what we eat! Listening to that fellow, you'd think he was worried about your organic vegetables making him sick! I think he did have something against organic food after all." With this bit of oratory, she buys half of what is left of my squash along with a couple of new potatoes as a show of support and good faith, and thanks me for my efforts in growing my food organically.

This Saturday morning ends, fittingly, if not amusingly with the growers packing up their goods and displays to go home and the last couple in the parking lot coming up to the back of my truck only minutes before noon. They're an older couple, and the wife turns to me after looking for a long time at the few yellow squash still lying there in the basket on my tailgate and says, as if she feels my expectant stare and owes me an explanation as to why she is not going to buy the squash, "We don't eat that much squash." As she begins to walk away, her husband turns to her and almost under his breath retorts, "I would if you'd fry it!"

The conversation and the tales at the tailgate market are as puzzling as they are endless, and as interesting as the food is good.

You Are What You Eat

If it's true that you are what you eat, then this week I'm blueberries, blackberries, cucumbers and new potatoes. It's been a "bumper" year for all four and my tongue is purple, my throat is cool, and my belly is full.

Here at the tailgate market, a young girl has shown up with a large beer cooler from which she is selling cottage cheese cartons full of the fattest blackberries you've ever seen. And Karen and Johnny White are selling them by the gallon. The blackberries will be the first thing to sell out, and soon the young girl will be over in the music tent playing fiddle tunes with Cathy Arps to a growing and enthusiastic crowd of listeners.

As I eat a handful of blackberries I have traded Karen and Johnny for some of the largest new potatoes I've ever grown, I'm reminded, again, of the old medicinal adage "You are what you eat." Like most precepts and folk wisdom, I've always wondered at the origin of this phrase, and just how literally we are supposed to take it. Are we, literally, what we eat? Common sense would lead one to believe that a healthy diet would produce a healthy person. But then, there are so many exceptions. People who can (and do) eat anything and are still slim, trim and vital, as well as those who eat well and are sick. But in the end, for most of us at least, I think that what we eat plays a significant role in our over-all mental and physical health. How could it not?

Here at the tailgate market we are mostly organic growers. We grow organically not because we can charge more for our produce (in fact, most of us are charging LESS than what you'd pay for radiated and chemically-induced produce at the supermarket), but because we believe in the old adage of "You are what you eat." We like the rich, sweet, even loamy taste of organically grown foods. And we like knowing what goes in and on the food we put in our bodies, of having some modicum of control over our lives. Those who buy our produce would seem to agree—including the many vegetarians we see each Saturday morning—those folks who have abandoned the American obsession with eating meat for every meal and have taken to a lighter fare and are leaner and meaner for having done so. There are no hogs being butchered or slabs of steak being sold here at the Sylva market— no "mad cows."

The "blackberry girl" and I are having fun imagining that today we ARE blackberries. We stick out our tongues at each other as proof of our identity and tell blackberry jokes we have made up on the spot. Of course there are the obvious allusions to chiggers, briars, and raccoon scat in our silly jokes, and we have fun passing the morning away with our happy childish banter.

A couple truck positions down from mine, a large crowd has gathered around the honey vendors from over in Almond. And much "bee talk" is going on. "Talk about organic!" I hear a loud male voice proclaim. And it's true, the bees give us one of the most wonderfully and miraculously natural products known to man. "Ambrosia," "food of the Gods," "the land of milk and honey" are just some of the maxims that have been handed down to us over the ages. And, if it's true that "man can not live by bread alone," then could he, maybe, live by honey, alone? With these thoughts wreaking havoc in my head, I wander over to the honey tent, make my way to the display table, and put a big plastic spoon of the early clover and wildflower honey in my mouth. MMmmmmmnn ... The blackberry girl is there in the honey tent, too. She has beaten me there and you can see some of her "free taste" oozing out of the side of her mouth and running down her chin. We smile at each other, knowingly. Now, we are honey!

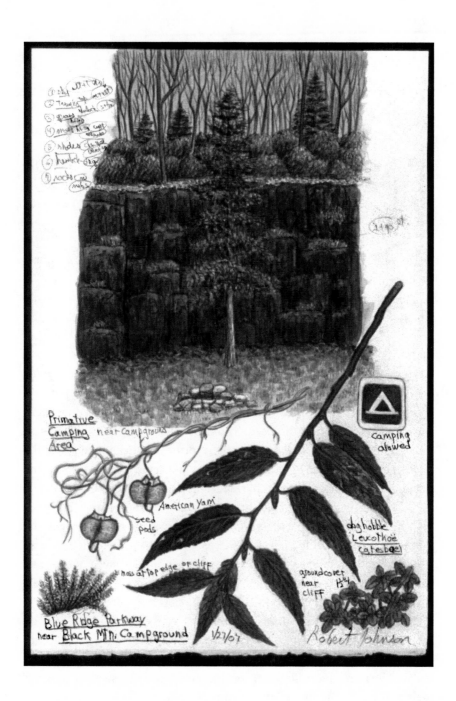

131

Coons in the Corn

We got some good rain this week and the corn and the okra are beginning to show up at the tailgate market. First corn of the season. A time, traditionally, for celebration. Roastin' ears. Corn-on-the-cob.

But the ripening of the corn brings problems just as it brings a warm satisfied satiety after supper. In a word: it brings the raccoons. Saturday morning, and before making my way, sluggishly, to the tailgate market by eight o'clock, I had been roused at 4:00 a.m. by the sounds of blue tick and red bone hounds out in the woods behind the house, where they'd treed a coon. (One knows these things by knowing the sound of the neighbors dogs and from a lifetime of experience). Already awake, my first thought (after silently cursing the dogs for having woken me up at such an ungodly hour) was of my corn patch—about halfway between the house and the tree where the two dogs were barking. Knowing that the corn would be ripe enough to pick and to take to the market to sell later in the morning, and knowing that the coons knew the same, I got out of bed and put on my robe, grabbed the flashlight from the bedside table and made my way out of the house and into the night. The dew on the grass was wet and cold—a shock to my feet as I stepped from the porch—but it woke me up and helped me make my way up the incline, into the pasture, to the corn patch. Just as I had feared, the sound of mandibles engaging fodder met my ears as I rounded the turn by the big pile of brush I'd heaped at the southwest corner of the garden. The coons were in the corn!

Oddly, my first thought at this moment was, "Damn them, how do they know when the corn is almost ripe?" Every year they seem to get to it a day or two before it's ready to be picked—too soon to harvest and yet just enough milky corn on the green cobs to sweetly moisten their pesky lips. But the point is, that they do know. They always know.

And there they were in all their masked and ring-tailed glory hovering over the timbered stalks.

Without giving away the ending to this little tale, let me, instead, say that I'll be getting up every morning for the next week at 4:00 o'clock a.m. defending my corn crop from the raccoons—much as I had to get up at first light back in mid-May in order to keep the new corn sprouts from the crows. (Or as the old timers used to say: "When the corn-planter bird squawks of a mornin' you'd better run to the field!")

Corn is a much sought-after commodity in the natural world, just as it is in the world of humans, as evidenced by how fast the fresh corn has disappeared from the back of my truck, today, here at the tailgate market. The group-mind of the buyers today is anticipatory, as every customer who comes by my station is looking for corn. And the spirit is generous and appreciative, as displayed by one of my regular customers who is so elated with the fact that I have brought corn to sell that she tips me an extra buck—the first time in my memory that I've ever been tipped for what I've grown! "I just love Silver Queen corn," says the woman as I fill her poke with the unshucked green heads. "There's nothin' better in this world!"

With corn on everyone's mind, the Sylva market is rich with tales of a-maize-ing grace. "They wanted $10 for a single sack of corn," I overhear an elderly woman saying to her friend as they buy potatoes from the man from Whittier whose new potatoes match the color of his aging, red Nissan truck parked next to mine. "Well, I would have paid $15!"

While the coons back in Tuckasegee gather to plan their next wave of attacks on the second planting of corn, here at the farmer's market we swap raccoon stories as we pack up our trucks at quitting time. Our pockets full of corn-fed cash.

Buying Locally

Things are hoppin' here at the tailgate market this week. With corn, tomatoes and beans coming in, the folks who have only been circling the market for the last month, have landed and have come in to check things out. With ole-timey fiddle and guitar music coming from the jam-session going on in the music tent as a fitting backdrop, the business of banter & barter goes on at each tailgate station.

"I'm bad to cook with fat back," I can hear one customer saying a couple truck-beds down the line. She is buying fresh cabbage from one of the vendors— "I just add a cup of water to the oil in the skillet and throw in the chopped cabbage for a few minutes, and it's done. Now, you talk about good!"

A large red SUV with Missouri plates pulls up along the curb in front of my truck, rolls down his window and shouts, "You got any peaches?" To his drive-in, drive-by approach I respond, "No, this is NORTH Carolina, South Carolina is down the road and to the right." He smiles sarcastically, and drives away.

Aside from the chatter, there has been a lot of talk today about the importance of growing and buying good food and the mindset of buying locally. I remember my old friend Zoro saying to me some twenty years ago, "Folks are livin' out of cans and pokes these days. When it's on the table it's not fit to eat!" He was talking about trucked-in, store-bought food and the advantages of a short, legible food chain as being preferable to refrigerated, long shelf-life foods coming from across the country and from other continents in various states of suspended freshness. Zoro believed that the best way to maintain quality in our diet and to keep the flow of currency in the community was to buy what we eat from growers close to home, and preferably to eat what one could grow themselves.

Maybe the best example I've ever encountered of the ideas of "buying locally" and community gardening comes from right here in our own community exemplified by Ron and Cathy Arps' *Vegenui Gardens* in the Cope Creek community of Sylva. Since the Arps and I are parked side by side today selling produce, and with a break in the action here at the tailgate market, we have found a chance to chat about their farm. "If there's any inherent wisdom to the '60's adage of 'thinking globally and acting locally,' it would certainly apply to the business of truck farming and the farmer's market," Ron says, beginning. "But my approach to what we are doing at Vegenui isn't really a philosophical one, but more a practical one. I am gardening because growing food is something I've always wanted to do and because I've found that I love this kind of work. It's a very hands-on approach and designed from the combination of experimentation, trial and error and common sense. I'm just doing what I've found that works for me. If there is any residual benefit, philosophically or ideologically, it's not because I'm trying to make a political or social statement, but rather that maybe we've hit on some things that seem to work, here."

Ron and Cathy Arps have lived in Jackson County since 1976 and have done a variety of things to make a living since that time and prior to embarking on their organic garden business. Vegenui (a word they've created combining the word "vegetable" and the New Zealand/Maori word for "big") Gardens is, essentially, a ¾-acre piece of bottom land fed by an above-ground spring, where a brilliantly simple concept is being implemented to give Ron and Cathy a means of support and to provide the community with fresh organic garden produce. Their method is to grow enough food for up to twenty families and to sell that produce in shares—giving a new meaning to the idea of "share-cropping!"

"Our customers buy either full or half shares ($450 for a full share, $225 for a half share) in the garden at the beginning of each year. In exchange, we grow and harvest the food—rationing it out equally amongst all the existing share holders—and then they come on the designated distribution days to pick up the food," Ron explains. "In this way, the members of our little cooperative venture share, not only in the bounty of what we produce, but in the risks of possible inclement weather, garden pests, a poor growing season, etc. as well. Having our customers, in a sense, owning a share of the garden, and having them coming to pick up their weekly portions, takes not only the worry out of the process, but a lot of the overhead in terms of having to set up a distribution system and to truck our produce to other parts of the county or region to sell. In this sense, we've got the best of all worlds. Some of our customers are so into this collaboration that they want to spend time in the garden themselves, working hands-on, weeding, or doing other sorts of chores. This way, they not only know where their food is coming from, but have the added experience and pleasure of having been part of the process of growing their seasonal allotment of 400 pounds or so of food—which, of course, as we all know, makes the food taste better," he says, with a wide grin. "And some of our custom-ers even occasionally bring us a cooked meal, so that we don't have to cook supper after working all day in the garden. This, of course, is a wonderful bonus!"

Happy to have put his book-keeping and income tax business be-hind him, and with his wife, Cathy, helping with the gardening when she's not teaching music lessons or performing in various orchestras and ensembles in the area, Ron brings his overflow produce to the Sylva tailgate market on Saturday mornings. This allows him to make a small additional income, but also gives him the opportunity to meet new people in the community who become potential share-holders in his Vegenui enterprise. "It gets me out of the garden and gives me something of a social life," he says. "Otherwise, especially during the growing season, I'm so busy with the gardens that I don't have time for much else. I'm pretty much there sun up to sun down."

Ron waxes philosophically about community, buying locally, and Community Supported Agriculture and the Carolina Farm Stewardship Association of which he is a member. "My mission is not only to produce good food, but to recycle things in the community. My tools, for instance, are made locally and I recycle beer boxes for mulch and horse-manure from Bill Kraus," says Ron. "I use what I can from the community—bottom ash that I get from Jackson Paper, and such. I like the idea of keeping the money here in the community, of re-cycling that as well. This process also puts me in touch with the various members of the community and what they are doing. The cycle of exchange, the sharing, is all a part of this idea of community-supported agriculture. And I suppose that there is even an element of teaching, of education, in this local give-and-take process. One of my customers came recently with one of her children— 'What's that?' the ten-year-old said pointing to my broccoli bed. She had never seen broccoli growing before and so she learned something that day. So, in general, I believe that people can improve their lives by supporting local farmers. There are health issues inherent here as much as there are social issues. There is such a big difference between what I grow and what people can buy in the store! My customers appreciate the freshness of the local produce. And in terms of the taste, there is no comparison."

"Amen!" chimes in one of Ron's customers who has been eaves-dropping on our conversation and has come out from hiding behind the cab of my truck. "Have you ever been up to see Ron's place?" she adds. "Why, it's a veritable Findhorn! I've never seen a more beautiful garden. I just love hangin' out there, it's so pleasant." Ron smiles as she goes on— "Have you ever tasted his carrots?" She picks up a bag of beautiful deep orange carrots from the tailgate of Ron's truck and puts them up to her nose. "And they smell so good! And my grand-daughters just love those purple beans. We're learning things all the time—like the free recipes Ron gives us, not to mention the free herbs and flowers that we are allowed to pick when we come to pick up our produce each week! It's not only a whole lot more fun than the super-market, it's a whole lot better. This is a very special thing to have here, and so close by!"

Ron, now, is blushing, as he hands his share-holder customer a fist-ful of cucumbers he has taken from the basket on his tailgate. "Here, take a few extra cucumbers with you—we've got extra cucumbers today."

While I know of no one else who is doing exactly what Ron and Cathy Arps are in terms of community-supported agriculture, the idea of buying locally is getting a great jump start here and at other farmer's markets around the region. What used to be commonplace and an organic part of local communities here in the mountains, has been lost to the rush for a quick-fix diet and social habits revolving around various technologies. With community agriculture and buying locally cut out of the social equation for almost a generation, people are beginning to perceive what they've been missing, and are showing up on a regular basis at the tailgate market.

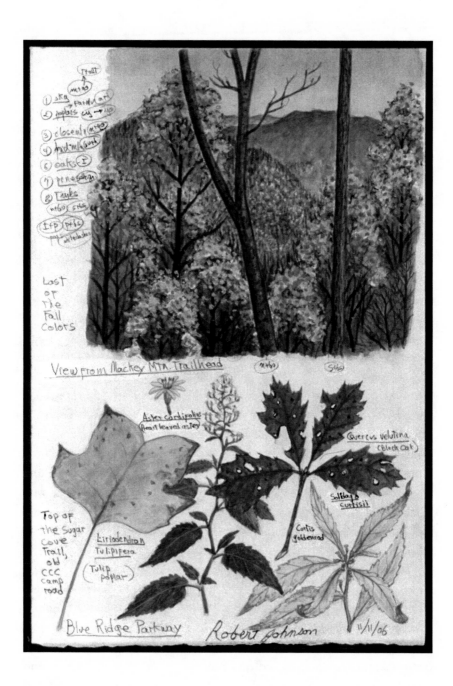

Fire and Rain

As I pulled my pickup into the tailgate market this past Saturday morning, I was met with the sound of sirens and the eerie glare of flashing lights and a parking lot full of trucks and cars. "Wow!" I thought to myself, "the word has gotten out and the farmer's market is a hit!" Unfortunately, it wasn't some sort of attraction gimmick and the hordes of early-bird shoppers that I had imagined, but rather Aquilla Green's old pickup had had a carburetor fire and the entire volunteer fire department was on the scene to put out the flames. An auspicious, if not fiery, beginning to what promised to be another hot August day!

As the fire department trucks and the various hangers-on disappeared from the scene and the growers and vendors began backing their vehicles up along the curb to set up their stations for the rest of the morning, a light, weepy mist began falling from a mizzly, gray sky. "Not a good sign," the vendors were saying to each other through the looks in their eyes. And I remembered an old mountain adage: "When raindrops gather like berries on the bushes you can bet your thumb there's more rain a-coming." But only the rain gods, Pluvius, Zeus, and Thor knew what was in store, weather-wise, for the rest of the day. Looking up at the sky, the only words that came to mind were words that I'd heard long ago as a child over in Graham County, "Yes, hits goin' to weather."

And "weather" it did. For the next two hours, and until almost 11:00 we got a steady, light Scottish rain. Not the "thundery weather" we'd been getting all week, not a "sizzly sod-soaker," or "nubbin' stretcher," as the elder generation of mountain folks would refer to it, but a "pretty good chunk of rain," none the less. As we all stood around our trucks in our slickers and rain ponchos watching our baskets and tailgates fill up with water, and wondering whether we should just call it quits for the day, a remarkable thing happened. People started coming to shop. Despite the dreariness of the day, customers began showing up, milling around, and buying produce. With this bit of unexpected good fortune, instead of packing up and returning home, we vendors hung in there, braving the weather as well as our earlier and equally dreary forecasts of a cat-and-dog day for sales.

While we were getting our "soft day," as the Irish call them, in Sylva, over in Madison County they were getting a real "Devil's foot-washer!" A brash of thunder-squalls and flash floods were filling the rain gauges. Most of the county was being transformed into a "moving road," or "a strong brown god" as T.S. Eliot called it in one of his poems. At the news of the rains over in Madison County, a customer who has been fondling my bushel basket of large Kinnebeck potatoes says, "That rain over there must be the effect of the men walking on the moon—or so Mama says. We've had so much rain around here lately, that what we need now is a good hard rain to settle the mud." I smile at her colorful speech and count my blessings that our spell of rain, here, is as siccative as it is.

It's been a good year, weather-wise, for us gardeners. After several years of draught and near draught conditions, any rain would have been welcome. We've had what I'm going to call an "ole timey" summer—with rain showers occurring almost like clockwork late in the after-noons— like what I remember when I was a boy here in the mountains. In those days there was a mountain superstition for rain-making that said: For a dust-settler, hang one dead blacksnake by the tail to a sassa-fras bush. For a gully-washer, hang two snakes. And for a sizzly sod-soaker, three snakes. We've not had to conjure the rain this year, and I've not had to irrigate my gardens at all. In fact, the pump across the road down by the river hasn't been cranked up even the first time. If anything, we may have had too much rain. But I'm not complaining, and here at the tailgate market we've all gotten a bit giddy, braving the rain today. To pass the time, Jackson County Agricultural Extension Agent Christy Bredenkamp has broken out her umbrella and is doing an impromptu song-and-dance version of Gene Kelly's "Singin' in the

Rain," with all of us vendors clapping and singing along in chorus. Our spirits warmed by our own foolishness, sporadic water fights, umbrella antics, and by the steady stream of customers that continue to come, we slosh on through the Scotch mist of the morning.

By eleven o'clock or so, the rain begins to back off. The tries to make its way through the clouds, and as soon as our slickers come off we realize that we've all but sold out of produce Despite the gout of rain that has been dribbling down all morning, we've had the best selling day ever! Who would have thought?! I am reminded of how, while living wild out in the woods along the Green River in Polk County, I learned to "read the signs" in the weather and could pretty much predict what would come. Would that we could predict good sales days here at the tailgate market in the same way! I don't think a one of us would have predicted that we'd have sold near this much produce, if any, by the end of this day. But we're not rain doctors or fortune tellers here, yet I suppose we've all learned a lesson today, and have become a little more proficient as neophyte, knee-jerk hyetologists.

As the customer crowd thins out and the pools of water around our trucks begin to evaporate from a now-strong, directly overhead noonday sun, and with our pockets full of change and cash, having stuck out this Saturday morning to the very end, we begin packing up our baskets, bags and scales. It's already after noon and Christy does one last version of "Singin' in the Rain" with a folded umbrella, tap-dancing in water still pooled in the gutter to sarcastic, good-natured applause, as Mrs. Green's truck starts up this time without fiery incident and rolls toward the street.

The Market As Midway

There's something for everyone at the tailgate market this week. With a real mix, now, of organic and non-organic growers bringing in their produce and goods, there are baked goods, herbs, soaps and salves, flowers, landscape plants, canned goods, honey, an expanded assortment of garden produce, and even watermelons from Neil Dawson's place over in Webster—and everyone is selling out. It's a hot, mid-August day and two young girls have set up a lemonade stand along the curb of "tailgate row" and are drawing some of the biggest crowds.

With the clock on the historic Sylva courthouse in its perpetual position of 12:00 noon, Harley's rollin' up and down Mill Street on their way to Cherokee, and the music tent back up and running after a couple wet weekends, Sylva is experiencing it's best week thus far for vendors and buyers. There is a festive feeling in the air and conversation is high-spirited.

Over at Molly Shaw's VW bus awning there's a lively conversation going on about her "Incredible Edibles." The hummingbird harvest is in an she's brought in her hummingbird bread. "No, my bread is NOT made from hummingbirds," says Molly in response to a customer's tongue-in-cheek question. "Oh, we thought that maybe it was kinda like blackbird pie, or something," the customer comes back, laughing.

Meanwhile, down at Becky Lipkin's station a crowd of women has gathered in dynamic conversation. "I'm puttin' that basil I bought here last week on my tomato sandwiches," says a slight, older woman who has been walking around the market all morning carrying two large shitake mushroom logs she's purchased from Christie Bredenkamp.

"I like my fruit just the day before the gnats get 'em," says another, slightly younger woman. And Becky replies, without hesitation, "I like mine that way too, but I like my corn when it's still got a little "pop" in it—like bitin' into a tick."

With the women's group "going on" next door, and "Tee Tee" from Florida in her white Sienna cruisin' the curb hoping to spot something from her car, I'm busy selling produce. "I've got everything you've got in my garden, "says a wisp of a man in a big green and yellow John Deere cap, as he purveys the baskets of vegetables positioned on my tailgate. "I've got all that, but I ain't got okra. I'll take everything you have." While I'm making change for the okra sale, I can hear Becky's voice rise above the animated buzz of the market noise and traffic. She's addressing a middle-aged woman who is walking up the sidewalk towards her truck with a tote bag in one hand and a large wad of money in the other. "I love to see folks walkin' around with money in their fists, ready to drop it," she says so everyone can hear. The woman flashing the greenbacks is drawn into Becky's crowd and emerges a few minutes later with a heather plant and a couple of the largest acorn squashes any of us have ever seen.

It's about ten o'clock and John Beckman from Unahwi Ridge Farms has unloaded a large catapult contraption from out of the back of his pickup, and he and Johnny White have manhandled it out into the street. With business coming to a screeching halt with the unveiling of Beckman's "Zucchini-pult," all eyes are on the action in the street. "This device was designed to take care of all those vegetables that come out of the garden that you don't want," announces Beckman like a carny barker. "All those volunteer squash and pumpkins from the compost pile. And this thing is also good for fast home deliveries," he continues as the crowd comes alive with laughter.

After a lively demonstration of his invention, and with the street alongside the railroad tracks littered with oversized, smashed squash, and everyone along the vendor's strip cheering, Beckman takes a few bows for the crowd and delivers his acceptance speech one-liner, "We know how to have fun down at the farmer's market!"

After all the hoopla has died down and business begins to pick back up again after the interlude, and elder man who is now standing next to me beside my truck and pointing over to the creek on the south side of the parking lot, says: "Why, you can launch that zucchini into the river for all I care! That's about all them things are good for."

Bounty

It's a rare, cool, cloudy day here at the farmer's market and "tailgate row" is full of vendors and the produce is plentiful. In fact, Sylva's Mill Street market this week is a virtual Horn of Plenty, a cornucopia of fresh foods, plants and related greenery. With local gardens and farms at the peak of their growing season, the only word that comes to mind to describe the plethora of product rolling into the market today is "bounty."

Last week it was the Harleys parading by on Mill Street, this week it's antique cars (old Chevys, Fords, Chryslers, Edsels ...) and the "god of gardens" has opened the flood gates. A couple of weeks ago it was the rain, this week it's the produce that is pouring in. Eugene Reed from Worley Farms over in Whittier arrived this morning with his truck-bed filled to overflowing with a hundred dozen ears of Silver Queen sweet corn—with the green shucks visible and blowing in the wind as he pulled into the lot. Selling for the best deal in western North Carolina at two dollars a dozen, customers have been hanging around his truck all morning like ants on sugar. Bounty!

"I got up at six o'clock this morning to pick this corn," Eugene says, wiping the sweat from his brow as he rakes his mound of corn toward the tail of the truck with a long-handled potato fork. "I couldn't hardly see what I was pickin' it was so dark at that hour. I've got to sell all this today, otherwise I'll have to work all the rest of the day just putting it up! So, I'm selling it at a good price." He stops talking long enough to sell three dozen ears, adding a gratuity of a few extra ears, to a young couple who walk away with big smiles—as if they can already taste the corn feast they will have at supper tonight.

Meanwhile, Neil Dawson has shown up with a big flatbed truck completely full of watermelons he's grown over in a patch he farms in Webster. I'd always heard that you can't grow watermelons up here in the mountains, but Neil has put an abrupt end to that fiction—with three different varieties of watermelon, all ripe, and ready to eat on the spot—which a couple of local children have already figured out as they make a mess of themselves and the pavement next to the big truck where they are noisily savoring the sweet, juicy fruit.

"There's nothin' to it," says Neil when I ask him about growing melons in the mountains. "I've got a big open field over there in Webster that gets sun all day. All I did was plant the seeds, scatter a little 10/10/10 around the hills, and walk away." Bounty!

While everyone's crowding around the Dawson's Green melon truck and the Worley Farms corn pile, Wilburn and Maxine Passmore from Ponderosa Farms over in the Green's Creek community have arrived in their blue Buick which they have backed up to the sidewalk to reveal a trunk full of old-timey cornfield beans.

"We sold our good Jersey cow, and our new chickens ain't a-layin' right now," says Wilburn, pushing his mountain fedora back a bit on his head. "So, we don't have sweet butter or eggs for sale today, but we've got several bushels of these good old cornfield beans." Immediately, there is a crowd and conversation going on around the back end of the Passmore car, and it's like old-home week, with folks greeting each other like long lost friends and catching up with tales about weather and their lives. Bounty!

Down the line a ways, Jim Parham and Mary Ellen Hammond have brought in their new crop of sourwood honey, and their display table is full of pint and quart jars glistening golden in the late-morning sun, as young and old, alike, huddle under their open-air tent tasting the warm honey on fresh-baked bread. Fellow beekeeper and garlic guru David Starr from the Union Acres community in Whittier is on the scene today and "bee talk" runs rampant outside the tent, while inside money changes hands. Bounty!

Everywhere I look, today, there is an abundance of beautiful food and groups of folks crowded around talkin' and tastin' and buyin.' By 10:30 the Passmore's have sold all their cornfield beans and are pulling out of the lot to return home to can beans. But just as soon as they've pulled out onto Mill Street, their vendor position is taken by the White's from over in the Love's Field community. With a big, broad-brimmed straw hat, Mrs. White is unpacking some of the most beautiful, big yellow tomatoes you've ever seen. Half-bushel baskets full of them. Bounty!

In no time she's joined by seventy-five-year-old Eulas McMahan who lives over on Green's Creek, and they're talking about tomatoes.

"I got the viniest tomatoes I've ever had," says Eulas. "Why, there is so much vine this year that I've been pickin' tomatoes off my roof!" Mrs. White smiles as I laugh and Eulas goes on.

"And I got tommy-toes, little red'uns and yeller'uns everywhere. The little girl down the road likes to come over and look in my garden. The other day I caught her in there eatin' them tommy-toes. Why, she was eatin' 'em afore they were ripe—eatin' 'em red and green, one after the other."

And if all this wasn't enough, toward the end of the morning I looked up from my lawn chair, which I had set out beside my truck, to see none other than the renowned Cherokee stone carver Amanda Crowe leaning up against the side of my truck and looking into the bed to see what I had left to sell. "I like that rock," she says, referring to a large piece of black granite I had sitting in the wheel well of my spare tire. "I'll sell it to you," I reply, smiling. "Everything's for sale, here, today," I tease.

"If that was soapstone, I'd buy it from you," she says in earnestness.

I get up and walk around to the other side of the truck where she is leaning on the sideboard and ask her how she is doing.

"I'm looking for blueberries and sweet corn," she says, eyeing Mary Jane Mrozkowski's almost empty five-gallon blueberry bucket sitting on a card table set up in the station next to mine. Amanda reaches into her shirt pocket and pulls out a little, flat, plastic case and opens it to show me what's inside. There are maybe a dozen miniature stone carvings of black bear cubs. Tiny in size, but done with precision and detail. Small signatures of her astonishing talent. Bounty!

It's been that kind of day at the tailgate market, a load of liberality and largess, graciousness and easy purse strings—with customers generously giving tips, and vendors pulling out of the parking lot with empty truck beds and money clips stretched to the limit. Eugene Reed's hundred dozen ears of Silver Queen are already being shucked all over Jackson, Macon and Swain counties. Neil Dawson goes home with maybe a watermelon or two for him and his wife, Peggy, for lunch. The Passmore's cornfield beans will be snapped and cooked tonight for dinner and canned tomorrow in a dozen pressure canners across the county, despite the August mid-day heat. And the bees over in Whittier and Bryson City will be back at work filling the comb cells robbed of their honey last week. Bounty....

150

The Guru of Garlic

While the weather at this week's tailgate market was overcast and gloomy at best, the mood on Mill Street in Sylva was anything but morose, as the first annual "Produce Pageant" was carried out by a respectable showing of growers and customers with a sense of playfulness and enthusiasm lasting all morning long. With categories including "most beautiful vegetable," "best personality," and "ugliest vegetable," entries were displayed on the sidewalk along a designated section of "tailgate row," where customers could vote for their favorites by placing a penny in baskets corresponding to each of the entries by this week's participating vendors. On display were shitake mushrooms, ruby chard, eggplant, bell peppers, tomatoes, watermelon, carrots, crook-necked squash, okra, marigolds, and ornamental and winter squash. With Pageant Master-of-Ceremonies Cathy Arps keeping things moving, and with the pageant's "Miss Congeniality," Autumn Demonet, soliciting voters, posing for photo ops, and keeping spirits high, ballots were cast (in truth, pennies were tossed), and with a total tally of 177 votes (or $1.77—which went into the donation coffers to help keep the Farmer's Market up and running) winners were crowned. For "most beautiful," the winner was an almost pink Neon variety eggplant; for "best personality," two spiral-entwined carrots; and for "ugliest vegetable," a wart-riddled and slightly decomposing Turban squash.

And what "Produce Pageant" would be complete without a visit from Mr. Potato?—who appeared mid-morning and human-scale in top hat and formal dress to the delight of all, especially the children, who followed him around all morning, tugging at his "skin"—reminiscent of scenes from the children's book *The Pied Piper of Hamlin.*

Out of the gala atmosphere and the Scottish mist of the morning emerged yet another character from local lore and farming fame, none other than the "Guru of Garlic" himself, David Starr, from over at Union Acres in Whittier. Setting his labeled display of exotic garlic bulbs out on the unused space of my truck's tailgate, we begin a conversation that escalates with each passing customer and lasts for the remainder of the morning—everyone having something profound to ask or humorous to say about the subject on display.

"There's no tale of epiphany as to why I began growing garlic, other than that I've always liked it. You can ask anyone I've known, and they'll tell you," David says, with a broad, suggestive grin spreading across his face. Not to let the perfect segue slip by, Neil Dawson from Dawson's Green Nursery over in Tuckasegee, who is talking with us, immediately picks up on David's statement, adding, "I used to work with an old fella, many years ago, who was bad to drink white liquor and eat fresh ramps—which was a deadly combination of the heat from the moonshine and the power of the ramps. Why, you could smell him coming from a hundred feet away!"

Meanwhile, a local man has slipped up to the tailgate of my truck and is looking closely at and fondling leaves from my basket of fresh-picked basil. "What's that?" he says, interrupting our little garlic convention and pointing to the basil and then taking up a handful and putting it to his nose. "Marijuana?"

"No, that's just fresh basil leaves that I picked this morning—good for throwing in your stir-fry or salad. But you can take some home with you to smoke if you like," I respond to his sincere question, with Neil and David laughing quietly to themselves in the background.

As customers come up to our tailgate covered, now, with bowls of the garlic cloves that David has brought to sell and to give, as samples, to the growers, they begin asking him a wide range of questions. He introduces each variety by focusing on its interestingly foreign or descriptive name. "There's 'Asian Tempest,' which lives up to its name and is the hottest kind of garlic that I grow. And there's 'Purple Italian Easy Peel' which, as you'd guess, is the easiest garlic to peel. And then there are varieties like 'Rocambule'—which always sounds to people like I'm saying 'rock and roll', so I just call it that. And then there's

'Nootka Rose'—which has a beautiful rosy hue to the peeled cloves and is one of my favorites, as it grows large, keeps well, and is not too hot so that you can eat it raw along with (Horn of the Bull) Mordello red peppers—which I also grow and which are a perfect compliment."

David Starr, who in an earlier incarnation was a librarian employed by the Sylva Public Library, is now a gardener/farmer and has been growing garlic in quantity (although not as yet commercially, as he says he hasn't quite figured out the most efficient marketing scheme) for four years. He grows seven varieties as a matter of course, and experiments each year with new and different varieties. "I'm always looking for the best varieties, those that do well here in the mountains," says David. "And I'm interested in keeping what I consider the best garlic alive and circulating. I save my seed and replant each year— strengthening the strain. All my garlic is grown organically, and I fertilize my crop with goat manure from my wife's Nubian goat herd.

"I use garlic in everything!" he continues emphatically. "It's an important ingredient in pesto," he says, pointing over at the basket of "marijuana" basil on our tailgate and laughing. "Garlic and olive oil is a great combination, and can be used in any number of ways—salad dressing, a *sautee* base, hot sauce for pasta or potatoes ... Why, I've even been known to eat garlic sandwiches!" he pronounces sincerely, almost blushing.

As he converses knowledgeably with customers throughout the morning—emphasizing that garlic is healthy, easy to grow, with no real diseases or pests to worry about and is a good companion plant as a deterrent to pests and disease, the supply of harvested bulbs dwindles to only a few, as people have been buying them to either enhance their Saturday evening meal or to plant this fall in anticipation of next year's crop of their own.

How Sweet It Is!

With the cool nights, the morning fog, and the hint of fall in the air, things at the tailgate market this week are moving at a slower pace. Even Johnny White's chickens are laying fewer eggs.

Though the frost is not yet on the pumpkin, most grower's gardens have peaked for the season. There are no more truckloads of corn, bushels of tomatoes, or trunks full of cornfield beans. No more of Neil Dawson's Webster-grown watermelons. Instead, Saturday morning at the Sylva market this week is dominated by those who have grown winter squash, root crops, and innovative canners and distillers of sweet liquids and salves. David Starr's garlic is back again and home-made jellies, jams, marmalades, sweet pickles are on display under the awning at Molly Shaw's "incredible edibles" spot on "tailgate row." Cathy Calabrese has her table full of fragrant flower essences, healing tinctures and salves. And further down the line, and the center of attraction today: the honey tent. Jim Parham and Mary Ellen Hammond have brought in their new crop of sourwood honey and their scented beeswax candles and their station is like a regular bee gum—with "the Honey Queen" little Shirley Temple-like Autumn Demonet in her blonde curls buzzing around the tent, carrying the "Local Honey For Sale" sign, attracting customers to the hive.

"How sweet it is!" Autumn says to one of the passers by, chanting the words from the black and gold sign she carries like a sign board. Too young to be "pourin' short sweetenin' into long" [wearing lipstick], Autumn dances up and down the sidewalk like the wind, a herald of the coming season which bares her name.

While the 'bee" tent is buzzing with business, and with "the boys of summer" about to become the "men of fall," those of us with little to sell are relaxing, talking about baseball to pass the time.

"What about them Cubs!" says one of the vendors parked on my left and sitting on the side of his tailgate, holding up a copy of USA Today that is open to the sports page. "This might just be their year. That is, if they can get past Seattle."

I nod enthusiastically, being an inveterate romantic and a lifetime Cubs fan, myself.

"And how about ole Sammy Sosa!" my neighbor goes on. "He's doin' it again. But I don't know if he'll ever catch that Barry Bonds fella. He seems awful strong."

I nod again, finally asking him what has happened to Mark McGuire.

"I don't think McGuire will ever catch Hank Aaron. He's got too many injuries, and that's going to slow him down," he replies, almost apologetically.

Meanwhile, Eulus McMahan has made his weekly appearance and has joined the men's group around the tailgate of my truck and joins into the conversation—adding some of his regional color and flair.

"I never played no baseball, but when I was a young'un we used to play a game we called *ante-over*. Hit was played with two people (or sometimes more), one on each side of the house. And we'd throw the ball over-top of the roof and the one or two on the other side would have to catch it—and them not knowin' where the ball would come from. After a while, Mama would get tired of hearing that ball bangin' up there on the roof and come out and chase us off. And we'd go off for a while, and then come back later and play it some more, until she chased us off again.

"I've got this big ole yard," Eulus continues. "Hit's one of the biggest yards up where I live. It takes me nearly two days to mow it. Last summer this ole boy comes up to the house one day, knocks on my door and asks me if'n he could play golf in my yard. I was a tad surprised, but I told him he could play his golf on my yard as long as he didn't knock the windows out of the house! And sure enough, a couple days later, there he was, out there in the grass playin' golf. Beats anything I've ever seen. I'm thinkin' now that maybe I ought to set me up a golf course in the yard. Stick some flags around, and a few sand boxes. That ole boy seemed to think it worked all right!"

We all laugh at Eulus's tale, as he leaves in a "swivvit"—his last words trailing off into the late morning as he moves on down the line of trucks and booths on Mill Street.

While the men have been musing about baseball, up the "row" in the honey tent, there's a "hellaballoo" goin' on as the women are exchanging recipes. With the ever-bare strawberries putting on their last blooms, Strawberry Honey is all the rage.

Strawberrry Honey Recipe

One pint of strained honey
One quart of wild strawberries
Heat honey in sauce pan over slow fire,
add berries, and stir until the two are
melded together.
Pour into jars.

One of the elder women in the group has just purchased a quart of the Nantahala couple's sourwood honey, saying "It won't be long before it will be time to make 'fruit' [applesauce], or 'sass' as my Mama use to call it. We're already pickin' early apples from our old tree. And they sure are sweet this year, 'specially for a tart apple. It sure has been a good year for 'sweetenin'!" she ends, with everyone saying yes and shaking their heads in affirmation.

All That's Green

Word from up the road in Tuckasegee this morning was that there has been a light frost. This news brings with it what most gardeners and farmers in Jackson County consider the end of the growing season. Aside from a few hearty vegetables, there is little that will, now, grow successfully here in the mountains. And so most of us will begin the work of tilling and plowing and sewing cover crops—in essence putting our gardens and fields to bed for another year.

However, here at the tailgate market, even with word of last night's frost, there are still growers bringing in some produce planted late, or fall crops planted early in August. So, there is still fresh and canned food for sale to accompany the nursery plants and herbs. Wearing long sleeved shirts and light jackets, today, as opposed to what has been lighter summer wear for the previous three months, the vendors keep warm with a constant chatter which continues on through the morning. I've been talking this morning with Neil Dawson, who has parked next to me in line on "tailgate row." We're talking about the nursery business and mainly the non-produce side of the farmer's market phenomenon. As noon approaches, and the vendors begin to pack up to go home, Neil invites me to come over to his nursery in Tuckasegee so I can see, first hand, what we have been talking about all morning. Fascinated by our conversation, I agree to go.

Dawson Green, the name of Neil and Peggy Dawson's Tuckasegee nursery business comes from the Irish euphonism *green*—which is a referent to *farm* or *field*. Neil's dad's farm down in LaGrange, North Carolina was called Dawson Farm and I've always wanted to use that name for a place of our own up here in the mountains," says Peggy as the three of us sit out in the 30 x 100 ft. main greenhouse of their operation located on the Tuckaseigee River near the intersection of where Highway 281 meets 107. "We've just changed *farm* to *green* because of the old-country connection and the reference to our green house business, and as a metaphor for the living things we produce. It has a certain charm, don't you think?" she says, with her familiar and slightly sarcastic smile.

Peggy leaves us to return to the house where she is busy preparing what will be ribs and hushpuppies for a benefit dinner for the Tuckasegee Volunteer Fire Department later in the day. As I look around me in the largest of the three greenhouses, I find myself surrounded by a great variety of hundreds of well-tended and displayed potted and hanging plants, as well as all kinds of accessory items, both functional and decorative. Proudly displayed near the front of the building is a large plaque which reads: "MidAtlantic Regional Garden Faire, 1st Place, Best Display of Plant Material."

In his fourth year of being in business for himself, and his twenty-fifth year living in Jackson County, Neil has been Farm Manager for Wolf Creek Tree Farm and Nursery in Cullowhee all that time—splitting his time, these days, between both businesses. As we walk around the greenhouse, Neil tells me about the business and answers my many questions.

"What we have, essentially, is a spring greenhouse operation—meaning that we open to the public for walk-in business by mid-March and continue until the 4th of July. The rest of the year we are open by appointment only. We are a 50% retail and 50% wholesale operation. This means that we sell to both retail businesses (such as farm supply stores and landscape nurseries) and to individuals. We have a full line of vegetables—much of which is grown as 'custom garden starters,' starting plants in flats for personal gardens—and annual flowers, as well as perennials and exotic species. Everything we sell is grown from seed or root stock, right here. It's a real hands-on operation. Greenhouse work is hard work and very time consuming. I've gotten a real education starting this business!" says Neil, wiping some imaginary sweat from his brow.

"I grew up farming. My background is mainly in tobacco and soybeans. I've used my knowledge of farming and soil science and applied it to my work with the Christmas tree business. I've also maintained a family garden for many years. My friends and neighbors and people from the community started coming over at some point and began asking to buy vegetables from my garden. Well, those humble beginnings led to what you see here, now."

As Neil talks, I am looking at a beautifully exotic orange-and-white flowering plant hanging overhead in a smoke-vine basket. I ask Neil what this plant is.

"That's a Siberian Iris. I call it the orchid of the iris world. We grow thirty to forty varieties of Siberian Irises. These kinds of plants, you might say, are my passion. The greenhouse operation all began with the small 10 x 20 ft. greenhouse out back. I've always had a love for orchids and exotic specialty plants such as tillandsias and rare irises. I'm a member of the American Iris, Orchid, and Siberian Iris Societies. In this sense, I guess you could say that uniqueness is our specialty here at Dawson Green. We've found that we can't compete with Walmart for flower-bed annuals, so our business, more and more, is focusing on perennials and exotic species. In addition to the orchids and irises, we grow and sell several different types of flowering ginger, tillandsia, banana plants, bog plants, ferns, and exotic and dwarf trees such as ginko, burning bush and Japanese maples. This is the direction our business is moving in, along with the herbacious perennials, or permanent plantings—such as hostas, phlox, columbines, etc....

"Largely, we carry what our customers want. And this is Peg's specialty—learning to read people and the market, and trying to be current with the coming trends, yet keeping the business one that caters to the community."

Having made our way through the three greenhouses and a large well-organized garden, we wander over to the house, where Peg is in the kitchen busy preparing for the Volunteer Fire Department dinner. On the wall above the stove is a wooden sign that says: "*Martha Stew-*

art doesn't live here!" Peg smiles as she sees me staring at her sign— her wonderful wit and sense of humor ever present.

"You boys getting hungry?" she asks, grinning sheepishly. "If it's ribs you're hankering for, you're going to have to wait," she says, and smiles.

As I ask her about Dawson Green, she talks while she kneads cornmeal dough for hushpuppies. "While the greenhouse business is a lot of work, I like the independence of working for myself. On the other hand, one has to be resourceful living here in the mountains. But I like the challenge of trying to spot the trends before they become trendy, if you know what I mean? And I like the process of providing things that aren't available at Walmart and at Garden Shows—things like smoke-vine baskets, rustic-made birdhouses and garden sculpture that com-pliment the greenery that we grow. This sort of thing is common fare here in Tuckasegee, but in the outside world these things are *objects d'art!* We've got people coming to us from as far away as Charlotte to get this kind of thing. All of these items are produced here locally, made by folks right here in the community. I like the idea of supporting the local economy, the community—of growing and selling locally. Keeping things close to home. This has always been a conscious im-perative for me in my end of the business. From seed to buyer, we're almost 100% local.

"Neil's talents are for farming, production. My interests are more people-oriented and in sales, so that's where most of my time is spent."

"Peg's more the people person of the two of us," Neil chimes in. "But I've been honing my people skills this summer at the Sylva Farmer's Market. I've enjoyed the comraderie there as much as the commerce. And I've come away from this year's market knowing what I need to concentrate on growing next year. I've learned that not every-one loves eggplant and okra," he says, smiling.

"There's always something we have to be thinking about even when we're doing other things, seems like. This afternoon, we'll be discussing next year's seeds, over ribs," Peg pipes in, laughing.

I use this opportunity to ask about the future. "What do you see in your crystal ball?" I ask Peggy.

"Two things," she replies without batting an eye. "Roses! And medicinal plants. Roses are making a come-back. Especially the new hardy varieties that will do well here in the mountains. As for the medicinal herbs and plants—I find that people are becoming more and more interested in learning about natural medicines and remedies. And I want to be part of the movement toward a more self-sufficient and natural health care system. Synthetic medicines are just too unreliable and expensive without the alternative of something more organic.

"While we want to expand and to change, we're going about it slowly. Learning as we go," Neil adds. "And we've enjoyed contributing to the Farmer's Market this year. I'm happy to see a market here in Jackson county. We've needed one for a long time, and it looks like it's been a success. It's been a good year down on Mill Street. And next year should be even better."

Planting Corn

When the moon
beds warm and silver in the sky, and
the signs are in the hands:

it's time to plant corn!

When crow starts
in spring with his breakfast songs
and cotton meal lies golden in the row:

it's time to plant corn!

Each row a line into space.
Each seed a hoop.
The smaller ends which meet
near the rhubarb bed, or
the ears of a god —

As the bluebird feeds
its first batch of young and
the sky takes earth in hand,
and we dance in the darkness of
a moonlit field where spring now rules the land
to the tune of Kanati's horn:

plant corn!

Acknowledgments

The author thanks the editors of the following journals, magazines, and newspapers where these pieces have previously appeared.

I.

Triple Negatives — *Now & Then, Salamander, Smoky Mountain News, Asheville Citizen-Times*
You Must Go Home Again — *Black Mountain Review, Smoky Mountain News*
New Native — *Katuah Journal, Smoky Mountain News*
Community — *Smoky Mountain News*
What Is Sacred — *Smoky Mountain News*
Overpopulation — *Smoky Mountain News*
Water As Archetype — *Heartstone*
Cold Mountain — *Wild Mountain Times*
No Dharma — *Bloomsbury Review, Smoky Mountain News*
The Last Luddite — *Smoky Mountain News*
The New Naturalists — *Nantahala Review, New Southerner, Smoky Mountain News*
May It Continue — *Heartstone, Zoro's Field* (Univ. of Georgia Press), *Poems From Zoro's Field* (Holocene Press)

II.

Road to Nowhere — *Smoky Mountain News*
It Can Happen To You — *Smoky Mountain News*
The End of Eden — *Sylva Herald, Smoky Mountain News*
What Next? — *Sylva Herald, Smoky Mountain News*
King Kong as Metaphor — *Sylva Herald, Smoky Mountain News*

The N.C. Land Rush — *Cashiers Chronicle, Sylva Herald, Smoky Mountain News*

Playing With Paradox — *Smoky Mountain News*

The Blue Wall — *Wild Mountain Times*

Stacking the Deck — *Sylva Herald*

Ask Not What Your County Can Do... — *Mountain Xpress, Sylva Herald, Smoky Mountain News*

The Idiot's Wind — *New Native Press* (broadsheet)

III.

Ain't Got Nothing — *Smoky Mountain News*

You Are What You Eat — *Elemental South* (Univ. of Georgia Press), *Smoky Mountain News*

Coons in the Corn — *Smoky Mountain News*

Buying Locally — *Smoky Mountain News*

Fire and Rain — *Smoky Mountain News*

The Market as Midway — *Smoky Mountain News*

Bounty — *Smoky Mountain News*

The Guru of Garlic — *Smoky Mountain News*

How Sweet It Is! — *Smoky Mountain News*

All That's Green — *Smoky Mountain News*

Planting Corn — *New Native* (New Native Press)

About the Author

Thomas Rain Crowe was born in 1949 and is an internationally-published writer and the author of twenty books of original, edited and translated works. He was a founding editor of *Katuah Journal: A Bioregional Journal of the Southern Appalachians*, which Gary Snyder called the best bioregional publication in the U.S.. His memoir *Zoro's Field: My Life in the Appalachian Woods*, written in the style of Thoreau's *Walden* and based on four years of self-sufficient living in a wilderness environment in the woods of western North Carolina from 1979 to 1982 was published by the University of Georgia Press in the spring of 2005, and is the winner of the Ragan Old North State Award for the best book of nonfiction in the state of North Carolina for 2005, as well as the Southern Environmental Law Center's Philip Reed Book of the Year Award for environmental writing, and a finalist in the Independent Publishers Book Awards for Regional Non-Fiction. He currently resides along the Tuckaseigee River in the Smoky Mountains of North Carolina. His articles, reviews and interviews have appeared in many prominent publications across this country and abroad. He has been a features writer for such regional publications as *Green Line, Wild Mountain Times* and the *Mountain Xpress*. He currently writes features, editorials and columns on culture, community and the environment for the *Smoky Mountain News*. As an activist, since 1979 he has been involved with such issues and organizations as The Canary Coalition (Clean Air), AMUSE (Artists and Musicians United for a Safe Environment), Project to Protect Native American Sacred Sites in the S. Appalachians, and has been on the board of the Southern Biodiversity Project, the Western Carolina Alliance, and the Environmental Leadership Council at Warren-Wilson College. His literary archives have been purchased by and are collected at the Duke University Special Collections Library in Durham, North Carolina. He lives in the Tuckasegee community in Jackson County, North Carolina.

About the Artist

Robert Johnson grew up in South America in Caracas, Venezuela. In 1964 he received an undergraduate degree at the University of Louisville in Louisville, Kentucky. From 1965 to 1967 he worked as an apprentice for Karl Knaths in Provincetown, Massechusetts, following which he studied with Mark Rothko before moving on to San Francisco and the Bay Area to become part of the counterculture and abstract arts scenes, where he went on to get a graduate degree in painting at Mills College in 1970. The west coast "back to the land" movement inspired him and brought him back to the east coast and to the Celo community in the Smoky Mountains of western North Carolina as part of a 1,200 acre land trust that was set aside in 1938 as an intentional community and where he has remained to the present day. His work has been described as "a blend of pantheism and Deep Ecology" with its focus on the "recording of our vanishing, wide-open natural environment." He has explored and painted ecosystems as diverse as those found in Badlands, South Dakota, Ecuador, Panama and New Zealand, while focusing primarily on the Southern Appalachian Blue Ridge region where he makes his home. His work has been exhibited widely in galleries and museums from Washington, DC to Georgia, and is collected in places such as the Asheville Art Museum, the University of North Carolina, Chapel Hill, and the Badlands National Park, in Badlands, South Dakota. He has painted murals on commission in several places in North Carolina, including the Raleigh-Durham Airport. He currently lives and paints in the Celo Community in Mitchell County, North Carolina.

Printed in the United States
124348LV00003B/169-216/P